Revolution

ANTHONY BURGESS was born in Manchester in 1917. After graduating from Manchester University, he served in the British Army until the end of the war, and then worked as a teacher and lecturer both in the UK and the Far East. He became a full-time writer in 1960 after being misdiagnosed as suffering from a fatal illness, and rapidly established himself as a prolific, witty and brilliantly inventive novelist. His many publications include *The Malayan Trilogy*, *Nothing Like the Sun*, *Earthly Powers*, *ABBA ABBA* and a quartet of comic novels about the dyspeptic poet F.X. Enderby. Burgess was also internationally famous as a reviewer, journalist, man of letters and broadcaster, particularly after the release of Stanley Kubrick's notorious film version of *A Clockwork Orange*; when not at work on novels, he also composed a great deal of music, wrote plays, screenplays and musicals, and proselytised for the study of linguistics. The recipient of countless awards and honours, he died in 1993, shortly after completing the verse novel *Byrne*.

KEVIN JACKSON is a freelance writer, broadcaster and documentary film-maker, whose productions include *Burgess at 70* (BBC, 1987) and *The Burgess Variations* (BBC, 1999). His previous books for Carcanet were *The Language of Cinema* and a collection of texts by Humphrey Jennings.

ANTHONY BURGESS

Revolutionary Sonnets

and other poems

Edited by Kevin Jackson

CARCANET

First published in 2002 by
Carcanet Press Limited
Alliance House, Cross Street
Manchester M2 7AQ

This edition, 2017

A CIP catalogue record for this book
is available from the British Library

ISBN 9781857546163

The publisher acknowledges financial assistance
from the Arts Council of England

Supported using public funding by

**ARTS COUNCIL
ENGLAND**

Set in Monotype Ehrhardt by XL Publishing Services, Tiverton
Printed and bound in England by SRP Ltd, Exeter

Contents

Introduction

Anthony Burgess, 1917–1993: English Poet

Poet? Well, many other things, to be sure: exuberantly fecund and original and various novelist; equally prolific composer of symphonies and ballet scores and musicals and quartets and fugues; witty, learned and much-published reviewer, biographer, journalist, critic; noted polyglot, skilled amateur of, and fervent advocate for popular education in, phonetics and other mysteries of linguistic science; inventor of primaeval languages (for Jean-Jacques Annaud's lavish caveman movie *Quest for Fire*) and of the Russian-based teenage sociolect 'Nadsat' (for a short novel, his most famous, about juvenile thuggery, the basis for a film by Stanley Kubrick which has been distorting his popular reputation for three decades now); habitual world traveller; energetic teacher and lecturer; translator; pub pianist; showman and television celebrity; highly paid screenwriter; internationally recognised *homme de lettres* on a Johnsonian or Edmund-Wilsonian scale, and author of some sixty published volumes, including the two-volume *Confessions,* which rank among the most sublimely entertaining and endlessly re-readable autobiographies in English.

But, also, yes: poet:

> *'Wachet auf!'* A fretful dunghill cock
>   Flinted the noisy beacon through the shires.
> A martin's nest clogged the cathedral clock,
>   But it was morning: birds could not be liars.
> A key cleft rusty age in lock and lock,
>   Men shivered by a hundred kitchen fires.

(The 'martin' is Martin Luther; the theme is the Reformation; the allusiveness typically Burgessian.)

Perhaps one should even say: first and last, poet. This claim might seem a perversely exaggerated one, since until this publication of *Revolutionary Sonnets and other poems*, only one of those threescore books listed on Burgess's increasingly crowded 'By the same author' pages was ever offered to the world as 'verse'; and that lonely volume, the long narrative poem *Moses,* found few readers and fewer advocates.

Burgess himself was always somewhat diffident in putting himself forward as a poet, even though one of his acknowledged masterpieces, the superbly funny quartet of comic novels about his (partial) alter ego, the dyspeptic bard F.X. Enderby, is crammed with original poems – not a few of which, including that one about Luther, had previously appeared in print under the name of 'Anthony Burgess', or (since Burgess's legal name, the name of his first four decades, was John Burgess Wilson) the initials 'J.B.W.'

Interviewed by the *Paris Review* in the 1970s, Burgess shyly admitted that he was sometimes tempted by the idea of publishing a volume of .Enderby's collected poems. 'I can see the sense,' he told his interviewer, 'of pretending that some one else has written your book for you, especially your book of poems. It frees you of responsibility – "Look, I know this is bad but I didn't write it – one of my characters wrote it..."' He went on to explain that his poetic ambitions, such as they were, would henceforward be confined to verse translations (he mentions *Peer Gynt* and 'Tcheckhov's *Chaika*', neither of which appears to have been completed, as well as 'a musical of *Ulysses*', which eventually emerged in time for the Joyce centenary as *Blooms of Dublin*). Poetry of the more conventional kind – lyrical, autobiographical – was not for him: 'too naked, too personal'.

Now, while not exactly disingenuous, these remarks do not quite tell the full story. It's true that the bulk of Burgess's work in metre – and that is a pretty sizeable bulk, since a *Complete Poems of Anthony Burgess* would easily run to several hundred pages – is written in the more or less impersonal modes of epic, drama, and translation, both free and precise. Yet the publication record shows that Burgess, far from 'knowing it to be bad', also took a touching pride in his slim body of highly wrought lyrics, and wanted it to be both read and valued.

In fact, there is a perfectly straightforward sense in which our author may be described as a poet 'first and last': he book-ended his career as a writer with lyrics. Apart from competition entries, letters to the editor and similar juvenilia, the very earliest literary productions of John Burgess Wilson were the short poems he published in Manchester University's student magazine *The Serpent* in the late 1930s. The last full-scale work Anthony Burgess completed, just months before his death, was the Byronic verse novel *Byrne* (published posthumously in 1995). His valediction, a lovely and immensely readable display of self-delighting virtuosity, is an unmistakably Burgessian compound of new and old.

He chose to say goodbye to the fleshly world in a demanding form he had never practised before: *Byrne* is composed mainly in mock-Byronic *ottava rima*, alternating with a modified Spenserian stanza, and it purports to be narrated by a self-confessed 'poetaster' named Tomlinson. But some of *Byrne* is in other metres. There is, for example, an epigraph of three enigmatic quatrains which decode the song of birds:

'Prudence prudence,' the pigeons call,
    'Serpents lurk in the gilded meadow.
An eye is embossed on the garden wall:
    The running tap casts a static shadow'...

There is a light erotic conceit, in a different quatrain form:

I have raised and poised a fiddle,
Which, will you lend it ears,
Will utter music's model –
The music of the spheres

And there are five rather cryptic, intellectually dense sonnets on the theme of revolution from Genesis to the Enlightenment:

Sick of the sycophantic singing, sick
Of every afternoon's compulsory games,
Sick of the little clique of county names,
He let the inner timebomb start to tick...

(The 'He', it soon becomes plain, is Lucifer; and this minor public school is Heaven before the angelic rebellion.)

To most of Burgess's admirers, these seven short poems were, are, at once recognisable as vintage F.X. Enderby. Quite a few readers would have recalled that he had also published them outside the Enderby books – notably in the autobiographical *Little Wilson and Big God* and *You've Had Your Time*, as well as in various small-circulation magazines. Now, a man who set scant if any store by verses he had composed more than thirty years earlier would hardly have troubled to embed them so prominently and so firmly in his *oeuvre*. (Burgess also enjoyed pointing out that T.S. Eliot, no less, had marked out 'Prudence prudence' and two other poems for special approval in a polite rejection note from his editor's chair at the *Criterion*.) However reluctant he was about laying claim to the grand title of 'poet', Burgess clearly cared a great deal for these miniatures, and did his best to see that they would be remembered.

I do not think he was mistaken in this. Without wishing to make inflated claims for his future place in the history of English poetry, I believe that, especially when judged as a whole, Burgess's poetry is (among other, not always fashionable virtues) not merely skilled but at times brilliantly inventive, not merely pyrotechnical but thoughtful, thought-provoking and, above all, richly entertaining. At the very least, he is – above all in his stage work – surely one of the funniest 'serious' poets of the last century, worthy of a place in the pantheon somewhere near, say, Richard Wilbur – and not too far away from those American verse entertainers like Ogden Nash, whom he once saluted in appropriate form:

I have never in my life said anything other than laudatory
Of the work of Ogden Nash, whose innovations were chiefly auditory,
Meaning that he brought a new kind of sound to our literary diversions
And didn't care much about breaking the poetic laws of the Medes and
    the Persians...

'Literary diversions' is a happy phrase: Burgess seldom forgot the Johnsonian wisdom that one of the two main obligations of the writer (better to enjoy life, better to endure it) is to give the reader pleasure.

I'd also like to underline the extent to which poetry was a major presence in much, if not almost all of his work as a novelist – which, incidentally, teems with poet-characters. Apart from the mock-heroic Enderby, there are the godly likes of Shakespeare (in *Nothing Like the Sun*), Christopher Marlowe (*A Dead Man in Deptford*), Keats and Belli (*ABBA ABBA*) representing the art at its most sublime, and, at the other extreme, a whole regiment of ghastly poetasters from Enderby's arch-enemy Rawcliffe, author of a single dud lyric 'in all the anthologies' via the twittering idiocies of Dawson Wignall and Val Wrigley in *Earthly Powers* to the artless Lloyd Utterage, splenetic advocate of Black Power and sullen attender at Enderby's creative writing class in *The Clockwork Testament*: 'It will be your balls next, whitey...' Even some of Burgess's most minor creations often give vent to some kind of lyric, as though Burgess simply could not keep the poetry from bursting out at the seams of his narrative.

Nor, at times, could he. As most readers will know, Burgess was always a 'poetic' writer in his novels – not, perish the thought, in the hack reviewer's sense that he wrote swooning purple passages, but more exactly because he exploited all those resources of syntax, diction, ambiguity and even punctuation (he was one of the twentieth century's grand masters of the parenthesis) that his more plodding contemporaries in the art of fiction usually neglected.

In this, he obviously took some cues from the modern novelist he most admired, James Joyce (his two introductory books on Joyce's use of language are outstanding, and his abridged version of *Finnegans Wake* a godsend for students). Less obviously, he had also paid attention to Ezra Pound – a poet he greatly respected, and could quote by heart even after a long evening of alcoholic refreshment. Pound had proposed that the three defining qualities of poetry were melopoeia, phanopoeia and logopoeia: the music of verse, the casting of images on the visual imagination, and 'the dance of the intellect among words'. Burgess, who suffered from poor eyesight, is a less phanopoetic writer than many, but in melopoeia and logopoeia he excelled. Sometimes, as in *Napoleon Symphony* (based on Beethoven's *Eroica*) or parts of *Mozart and the Wolf Gang*, he took the Paterian aspiration towards the condition of music about as far as intelligibility permits:

> The squarecut pattern of the carpet. Squarecut the carpet's pattern. Pattern the cut square carpet. Stretching from open door to windows. Soon, if not burned, ripped, merely purloined, as was all too likely, other feet would, other feet would tread. He himself, he himself, he himself trod in the glum morning. From shut casement to open door and back, to and to and back. Wig fresh powdered, brocade unspotted, patch on cheek new pimple in decorum and decency hiding, stockings silk most lustrous, hands behind folded unfolded refolded as he trod on squarecut patterns softness...

(Compare Mozart's K.550, first movement.) That, no doubt, goes a little too far; but there are many other occasions when a wedding of extravagantly mellifluous phrasing with dark matter comes off triumphantly well – for those, at any rate, with a taste for a prose thickened with allusion and made tart with all the resources of Burgess's famously hypertrophied word-hoard. A sample, chosen more or less at random, from the final chapter of *Nothing Like the Sun,* written in an allusive, punning hybrid of the language spoken by the subjects of Elizabeth I and that familiar to Elizabeth II's people :

> Let's swell a space on the irony of a poet's desperately wringing out the last of his sweetness while the corrosives closed in. It was she, though, the goddess, unseen as yet but stirring and kicking like a foetus, that dictated the titles, for this was indeed much ado and that what they willed and the other as they liked it. Meanwhile that bud I carried opened like a pomegranate, the roseate macules and papules blossomed and later grew to a hint of delectable copper – coins over my body, the hint of a leopard's (not a tiger's) hide. When it left, it left a stain as of dirty eaters. All my parts must be hoarse parts (thou wilt make a ghost yet, see if though wilt not, that is a very graveyard voice)...

Not to everyone's taste, this heavy stew? Decidedly not: Burgess was often accused of schoolboyish or schoolmasterly showing off, just as Enderby was routinely patronised or declared hopelessly *passé* by the critics ('Enderby's addiction to the sonnet-form proclaims that the 'thirties are his true home...'). Those of us who do warm to it are responding to its qualities of zestful excess, of Burgess's word-man's relish for the 'delectable' flavours in which fine language may dress and make piquant the most sordid subject matter (syphilitic sores), of a composer *manqué*'s ambition to use the full orchestral resources of English rather than just the odd squeak or toot of piccolo or cello.

Yoked together with this astonishing vitality is, almost always, an exacting sense of medium. In one of his rare moments of self-assertion, Enderby says 'I stand for form and denseness. The seventeenth-century tradition modified.' Though Enderby does not spell out the allegiance at greater length, it is clear that he wishes to be numbered alongside the generation of poets who, taking their cue from Eliot, were enraptured by the recently revived Metaphysicals, and wished to apply the tunes and conceits of Donne and Herbert to contemporary experience. Put another way, Enderby is, *toutes proportions gardées*, something of a William Empson, with perhaps a jigger or two of Robert Graves (the goddess mythology) and W.H. Auden for good measure.

The Eliotic/Empsonian strain remained deep in all of Burgess's lyrics until he was well into his forties. With fame came the possibility of new kinds of public voice: hence Burgess the poetic editorialist, treating readers of the *New York Times* and other publications to metrical musings on the Apollo project or the State of the Union; Burgess the composer of verse letters; Burgess the dabbler in epic. In all of this public verse, he becomes a much more eighteenth- than seventeeth-century figure, preaching the virtues of reason and tolerance in an age of violence and the widespread worship of irrationality. For the most part, alas, these poems are more polished than memorable.

But fame, and more mature years, brought on two great liberations in his verse writing. The first was more or less accidental: marriage to an Italian wife, and residence in Rome, brought him in touch with the extraordinary work of Giuseppe Gioacchino Belli (1791–1863), whose thousands of sonnets in Roman dialect – many on sacred themes – are an astonishing, and all-but-untranslatable combination of scatology and lyricism. Burgess set himself to translating some 70 or them, and then (for it is hard to make money from poems, and Burgess was a *professional* writer, one who writes for pay) composed a short novel in which they could be sold on the open market. Had he written no other verses but his Belli translations, Burgess would have been worthy of consideration as a poet of exceptional gifts.

The other liberation was a happy by-product of his fame. The better-known Burgess grew, the more the invitations poured in – not only to write articles or give lectures, but to write screenplays, to translate and adapt for the stage (operas and musicals as well as classical dramas such as *Oedipus the King*), to dream up original plays of his own. This flood of commissions helped sharpen two of his already keen skills. First, it honed the kind of metrical dexterity which allows the jobbing lyricist to fit words to pre-existing music with consummate neatness – to rewrite, for example, *Freude, schone Gotterfunken* both straight –

> Joy, thou glorious spark of heaven,
> Daughter of Elysium...

And not-so-straight:

> Do not be a clockwork orange,
> Freedom has a lovely voice.
> Here is good, and there is evil –
> Look on both, then take your choice...

Smart enough work for most, but still not quite smart enough for Burgess, who from his youth had been a keen admirer of all manner of popular songs (his mother had been in the music halls, his father played the piano in cinemas during the silent era), but above all a devotee of the great American wits and dandies of the form: Irving Berlin, Ira Gershwin, Cole Porter and, supremely, Lorenz Hart. Burgess's admiration for Hart was sincere, profound and enduring; he loved the sheer audacity with which Hart could conjure a rhyme from an apparently rhymeless phrase, or cram more internal rhymes into a couplet than might seem humanly possible – 'beans could get no keener re-/ception in a beanery' (from 'Mountain Greenery'), and the like.

In his memoir of a lifetime as a Sunday composer, *This Man and Music*, Burgess offers a small tribute to Hart in the form of some rhymes on the unrhymable word 'fugue':

> A concert, Hugo?
> By all means *you* go,
> But the very first note of a fugue o-
> presses me, like all polyphony.
> I'd rather have a diamond from Tiffany.

Burgess's translations for the stage – *Cyrano*, *Carmen*, *Oberon* and all the others – are chock-full of such inner rhyming and false rhyming, and amount to compact anthologies of audacious, or sometimes outrageously corny, tricks of sound:

> Warm full-blooded life:
> Women as shining as goddesses
> Under the bustles and bodices,
> Scent you could cut with a knife.
> Warm full-blooded life:
> Frilly silk drawers that have legs in them,
> Omelettes with five hundred eggs in them,
> Sherry and cream in the trif-
> Le.
>
> (*Blooms of Dublin*, Act One)

If William Empson is the presiding spirit of early Burgess, then Lorenz Hart rules over his later work for the stage; and Burgess would surely have growled at any literary snob who felt that there was something bathetic in that progress. (One hastens to add that he was not an inverted snob, either: among the most vile of his poetasters is the loutish 'Yod Crewsy' – loosely modelled on John Lennon, and, curiously, the victim of a mock assassination attempt on the page almost two decades before Mark Chapman squeezed his trigger outside the Dakota). Burgess's position was that a true lover of language will know how to find the joy in any skilled manipulation of its formal properties, whether mandarin like Empson's or popular like Hart's.

Pleasures both demotic and recondite abound in the pages of *Revolutionary Sonnets*; again and again in the course of editing I found myself unexpectedly smiling, chuckling and sometimes laughing out loud at some new felicity or feat. The point is central enough to be worth stressing again: thanks in part to the discipline of the market, Burgess never forgot that it was his job to entertain a reader or a listener who might be bored, distracted, careworn; and it is clear that he also wrote to entertain himself, keeping his own demons (they were many) at bay through the exercise of virtuosity. Was he a great poet? In the final analysis, perhaps not; I leave the verdict to others. But I have no doubt that he was a great entertainer and a wonderful writer. His gift for poetry was an essential part of that wonder.

A Note on the Present Text

I hand the daunting task of editing *The Complete Poems of Anthony Burgess* on, with all good wishes, to the as yet unborn scholar of the twenty-second or twenty-third century who finally has the nerve to tackle it. In the meantime, the reader will find in these pages:

(i) Almost all the shorter poems of F.X.Enderby; though not fragments from his early epic *The Pet Beast,* nor his later work on the conflict between Pelagius and St Augustine; nor the other squibs and fragments he produces; nor, alas, such exuberant feats of literary ventriloquism as his impromptu 'quotation' of verses by the minor Elizabethan dramatist 'Gervase Whitelady':

> So the world ticks, aye, like to a tocking clock
> On th' wall of naked else infinitude,
> And I am hither come to lend an ear
> To manners, modes and bawdries of this town
> In hope to school myself in knavery...

(ii) All but one of the early poems of John Burgess Wilson. The exception is a poem entitled 'Wir Danken Unserm Fuhrer', which has been removed at the request of the Burgess estate. Part of this poem can, however, be found in *Earthly Powers*, Chapter 54, where it is re-assigned to the Poet Laureate Val Wrigley. (The narrator comments that it gave Wrigley's reputation a considerable boost, since the Nazis took its blisteringly sarcastic praise of Hitler for the real thing, thus proving themselves not merely evil but remarkably stupid.)

(iii) All – or, more exactly, as much as I have been able to unearth – of the occasional and fugitive verse published under the name Anthony Burgess.

(iv) Representative selections from *Moses*, and from the plays and operas Burgess translated, and from the musicals he wrote for the stage or the page.

The Burgess fan will immediately note some obvious omissions. This selection does not include any of *Byrne*, which is still easily available in many bookshops; nor does it reproduce any of the seventy-odd translations of Belli from *ABBA ABBA*, since that volume is also still in print. In the latter case, I have chosen instead to return to the versions of ten poems by Belli which Burgess published in journals before the novel appeared.

There are some other, less glaring omissions, which are due either to lack of space, lack of editorial enthusiasm, or simple misjudgement. Among many other possible candidates, I have excluded: the 'Epistle to the Reader' from *Napoleon Symphony*, and the verse riddles sprinkled throughout *MF*, such as:

> Behold the sheep form side by side
> A Teuton roarer of the pride.
> [Behold = *Lo*; sheep = *ewe*; *Loewe* is German for Lion.]

as well as the cod-surrealist droolings of 'Sib Legeru' from that novel:

> London Figaro infra pound
> Threejoint dackdiddy Solomon
> Delay delay thou Gabriel hound
> Mucklewrath IHS brilliging on...

What else has been dropped? Assorted poems by characters in the *Malayan Trilogy* ('In moments of crisis hunger comes...'; 'Land where the birds have no song...'); the collected lyrics of Kenneth Toomey from *Earthly Powers*; Burgess's proposed improvement to a new translation of the *Rubaiyyat* by Robert Graves:

> (I see the book of early glory close,
> The green of Spring make room for winter snows.
> The cheerful bird of Youth flutters away –
> I hardly notice how it comes or goes.)

And much, much else besides. Provided the reader knows that the selection published here is a necessarily partial gleaning from a much larger field, no real harm will be done. Or so I hope.

A Personal Note

Editing Anthony Burgess's poems has been a small act of piety as well as a pleasure. Much as I am sometimes tempted to boast otherwise, I cannot really claim to have known him well, let alone to have been his friend; Burgess was given, anyway, to describing himself as a man without friends.

But I did spend quite a while in his close company in the 1980s and early 1990s, and at least two of these meetings (one in Venice, 1987, when I directed 'Burgess at 70' for BBC2, and the other in 1992, when I joined him on the British promotional tour for *A Mouthful of Air*) allowed me to express something of the gratitude I felt to him for years of instruction and delight. A surprisingly diffident man for one so frequently accused of being a terrible show-off, he responded to my embarrassed thanks with equally embarrassed courtesy.

What I had tried to convey to him, however clumsily, was his enduring presence in my life as a sort of inspiring imaginary uncle figure; a kindly spirit, distant yet constant, who not only cheered me through my adolescent and post-adolescent glooms, but hinted to me what I really should know about if I wanted to be properly, instead of just officially, educated. (Following up the suggestions in *Urgent Copy*, his first collection of literary journalism, was like an interdisciplinary A-level in its own right, in which Lévi-Strauss and Wagner hob-nobbed with Flaubert and Chomsky.) Three decades later, I still find myself habitually reaching into my private Burgess pile – not quite the complete set of three-score volumes, but only a few light – for the ever-reliable relief of hearing his witty, generous, encouraging voice, and for a reminder of the inexhaustible relish he took in literature of all sorts and conditions.

I am not entirely sure how his reputation will stand in the early twenty-first century: many authors experience something of a dip in the first decade or so after their death, and even Burgess may not be exempt from this routine fluctuation of stock. Already there are rumours of at least one antagonistic biography, and there has been some predictably ignorant broadsheet gossip-mongering about the man they invariably call the '*Clockwork Orange* author'. Vile as such phenomena are, they chime curiously with one of Burgess's recurrent themes – that of the vulnerable idealist (Enderby, Cyrano de Bergerac) derided and hounded by the cynical.

In small ways – through articles, in the two-part BBC film *The Burgess Variations* (directed by David Thompson, 1999) and now with the *Revolutionary Sonnets* – I have tried to serve Burgess's memory more appropriately. The verses gathered here can stand as yet another proof of his prodigiously fertile mind; I would also like to place on record my first-hand experience of him as a considerate, charming and, at heart, modest man: a *good* man. The last time I spoke to him, we were seated together on a flight back from Edinburgh to London. Three days earlier, he had been diagnosed with the lung cancer that eventually killed him. At my prompting – I had recalled a passage near the end of *You've Had Your Time* – he recited from memory some of his favourite verses, by Coventry Patmore.

They are sentimental verses (Burgess the arch-modernist was also an unashamed traditionalist), about a young widower who strikes his son in anger, then, remorseful, visits the sleeping boy and sees how, to solace himself, the lad has put his toys in order on a bedside table – 'ranged there with careful art to comfort his sad heart'. Patmore's poem is, of course, about poetry, and its real if fragile power to help make sense of misery and loss. Burgess spoke of himself as a man of constant sorrows who, unfathomably, seemed to the world at large to be a wag and a wit. His poems were among the wonderful playthings he produced both for his comfort and for ours: his toy, his dream, and (let us pray) his rest.

KEVIN JACKSON
July 2002

REVOLUTIONARY SONNETS

and other short poems by John Burgess Wilson, Anthony Burgess and F.X. Enderby

Sick of the sycophantic singing, sick
Of every afternoon's compulsory games,
Sick of the little cliques of county names,
He let the inner timebomb start to tick,
Beating out number. As arithmetic
The plot took shape – not from divided aims
But short division only. Then, in flames,
He read: 'That flower is not for you to pick.'

Therefore he picked it. All things thawed to action,
Sound, colour. A shrill electric bell
Summoned the guard. He gathered up his faction,
Poised on the brink, thought, and created hell.
Light shimmered in miraculous refraction
As, like a bloody thunderbolt, he fell.

Published as the first of 'Five Revolutionary Sonnets' in *Transatlantic Review*, 21 (Summer 1966), pp.30–2. Re-ascribed to F.X. Enderby in *Enderby Outside*, Part Two, Chapter Three, section 3. On the last line: "'That *bloody*," Enderby said. "It's really meant to express grudging admiration. But that only works if the reader knows I've taken the line from Tennyson's poem about the eagle.'" Also reprinted at the end of *Byrne* (1995).

I

Bells broke in the long Sunday, a dressing-gown day.
The childless couple basked in the central heat.
The papers came on time, the enormous meat
Flowered in the oven. On deep carpets lay
Thin panther-kittens, locked in clawless play.
Bodies were firm, their hair clean and their feet
Uncalloused. All their wine was new and sweet.
Recorders, unaccompanied, crooned away.

Coiled on the rooftree, bored, inspired, their snake
Crowed in Black Monday. A collar kissed the throat,
Clothes braced the body, a benignant ache
Lit up a tooth. The papers had a note:
'That act may mean an empire is at stake.'
Sunday and this were equally remote.

Published as the second of 'Five Revolutionary Sonnets' in *Transatlantic Review*, 21 (Summer 1966), pp.30–2. Ascribed to F.X. Enderby in *Enderby Outside,* Part One, Chapter One, section 2. Enderby's psychiatrist, Dr Wapenshaw, has discovered this 'treacherous effusion' in the cisatlantic journal *Confrontation* (just a smack at *Encounter*, presumably) and takes it as evidence that his patient, apparently cured of versing, has secretly slipped back to his bad old ways. Also reprinted at the end of *Byrne* (1995).

A dream, yes, but for everyone the same.
The mind that wove it never dropped a stitch:
The absolute was anybody's pitch,
For, when a note was struck, we knew its name.
That dark aborted any urge to tame
Waters that day might prove to be a ditch
But then was endless growling ocean, rich
In fish and heroes till the dredgers came.

'*Wachet auf!*' A fretful dunghill cock
Flinted the noisy beacon through the shires.
A martin's nest clogged the cathedral clock,
But it was morning: birds could not be liars.
A key cleft rusty age in lock and lock,
Men shivered by a hundred kitchen fires.

Written in the early 1950s. Published as the third of five 'Revolutionary Sonnets'
in *Transatlantic Review*, 21, Summer 1966, pp.30–2. Ascribed, with slight varia-
tions, to F.X. Enderby in *Inside Mr Enderby*, Part One, Chapter Three, section 2,
where it is read aloud by Vesta Bainbridge, to whom Enderby explains that it is
about the Middle Ages and the coming of the Reformation, the 'martin' of the sestet
being Martin Luther. Also reprinted at the end of *Byrne* (1995).

They lit the sun, and then their day began.
What prodigies that eye of light revealed!
What dusty parchment statutes they repealed,
Pulling up blinds and lifting every ban.
The galaxies revolving to their plan,
They made the conch, the coin, the cortex yield
Their keys, and in a garden, once a field,
They hoisted up a statue of a man.

Of man, rather: to most it seemed a mirror;
They strained their necks with gazing in the air,
Proud of those stony eyes unfilmed by terror.
Though marble is not glass, why should they care?
Later the time for vomiting the error:
Someone was bound to find his portrait there.

Published as the fourth of 'Five Revolutionary Sonnets' in *Transatlantic Review*, 21 (Summer 1966) pp.30–2. Ascribed, with a few minor variants, to F.X. Enderby in *Enderby Outside*, Part One, Chapter Three, sections 3 and 4, where it springs unbidden and inconveniently into his mind while he is in the middle of the act of love (to him, quite unfamiliar) with a Miss Boland, who is understandably distressed by his sudden scramble for paper and pen. Enderby glosses his new creation for his own benefit: 'It seemed pretty clear, really. This was what happened in a humanist society. The Garden of Eden... was turned into a field where men built or fought or ploughed or something. They worshipped themselves for being so clever, but then they were all personified in an autocratic leader... Humanism always led to totalitarianism. Something like that, anyway.' Also reprinted at the end of *Byrne* (1995).

Augustus on a guinea sate in state,
    The sun no proper study but each shaft
    Of filtered light a column: classic craft
Abhorred the arc or arch. To circulate
(Language or blood) meant pipes, and pipes were straight.
    As loaves were gifts from Ceres when she laughed,
Thyrsis was Jack. Crousseau on a raft
Sought Johnjack's rational island, loath to wait

Till sun, neglected, took revenge, so that
    The pillars nodded, melted, and were seen
As Gothic shadows where a goddess sat.
    For, after all, that rational machine,
Granted to all men by the technocrat,
    Chopped logic and became his guillotine.

Written 1959, when Burgess was in hospital undergoing neurological tests for a suspected cerebral tumour: one of his doctors, baffled by the poem's rather cryptic allusions to the orgins of romanticism in classicism, took it as grim evidence of mental disorder. Published as the fifth of 'Five Revolutionary Sonnets' in *Transatlantic Review*, 21 (Summer 1966) pp.30–2, which, among other significant variants gives, as above, 'Crousseau' – a conflation of Robinson Crusoe and Jean-Jacques Rousseau – for the otherwise baffling 'Caruso' of the text cited in *Little Wilson and Big God*. (Other substantial changes include *TR*'s 'sat up straight' for *LWBG*'s 'sate in state'; '(Blood or ideas)' for '(Language or blood)'; and 'Granted to Jack's tribe' for 'Granted to all men'. Re-ascribed to F.X. Enderby in *Enderby Outside*, Part Two, Chapter Two, section 1 and Chapter Three, section 2, where the poet attempts to explain his meaning – 'What I have to do is to show that romantic curves are made out of classical straightness' – and his bossy, newly arrived young Muse-figure takes a dim view of its craftsmanship: 'These lines are a bloody disgrace.' Also reprinted at the end of *Byrne* (1995).

In this spinning room, reduced to a common noun,
> Swallowed by the giant stomach of Eve,
The pentecostal sperm came hissing down.

I was no one, for I was anyone,
> The grace and music easy to receive,
The patient engine of a stranger son.

His laughter was fermenting in the cell,
> The fish, the worm were chuckling to achieve
The rose of the disguise he wears so well.

And though, by dispensation of the dove,
> My flesh is pardoned of its flesh, they leave
The rankling of a wrong and useless love.

Attributed to F.X. Enderby in *Enderby Outside*, Part One, Chapter Two, Sections
4 and 5: most of it comes to Enderby as he sits crouched in the W.C. of a train
from the South Coast to Victoria (with one main variant: 'I was nowhere, for I was
anyone –' (*IME*) in place of 'I was no one, for I was anyone,'). This is one of
the three poems 'mildly approved' by T.S. Eliot when he returned John Wilson's
unsolicited manuscript of verses in the mid-1950s.

'Prudence prudence,' the pigeons call,
    'Serpents lurk in the gilded meadow.
An eye is embossed on the garden wall:
    The running tap casts a static shadow.'

'Caution caution,' the rooks proclaim,
    'The dear departed, the weeping widow
Will meet in you in the core of flame:
    The running tap casts a static shadow.'

'Act! Act!' the ducks give voice,
    'Enjoy the widow in the meadow.
Drain the sacrament of choice:
    The running tap casts a static shadow.'

Written early 1950s. Re-ascribed, with minor variations (including 'Scorpions' for line 2's 'Serpents', and 'island' for line 3's 'garden') to F.X. Enderby in *Inside Mr Enderby*, Part One, Chapter One, section 5. For the purposes of the novel, the mysterious 'widow' – in real life, Burgess never, so he claimed, quite understood who she was – proves to be Vesta Bainbridge. This short poem was one of three marked for special approval by T.S. Eliot when he politely rejected a volume of poems which Burgess (then known as John Wilson) had submitted to Faber and Faber. Burgess seems to have been particularly attached to this poem, and used it as the epigraph to his final work, the verse novel *Byrne* (1995) – where, once again, it is attributed to 'F.X.E.'.

Shrewsbury, Shrewsbury, rounded by river
    The envious Severn like a sleeping dog
That wakes at whiles to snarl and slaver
    Or growls in its dream its snores of fog.

Lover-haunted in the casual summer:
    A monstrous aphrodisiac,
The sun excites in the noonday shimmer,
    When Jack is sweating, Joan on her back.

Sick and sinless in the anaemic winter:
    The nymphs have danced off the summer rout,
The boats jog on the fraying painter,
    The School is hacking its statesmen out.

The pubs dispense their weak solution
    The unfructified waitresses bring their bills,
While Darwin broods upon evolution,
    Under the pall of a night that chills

But smooths out the acne of adolescence
    As the god appears in the fourteenth glass
And the urgent promptings of tumescence
    Lead to the tumbled patch of grass.

Time and the town go round like the river,
    But Darwin thinks in a line that is straight.
A sort of selection goes on forever,
    But no new species originate.

Ascribed to F.X. Enderby in *Enderby Outside*, Part One, Chapter Three, Section 3.

To Tirzah

You being the gate
Where the army went through,
Would you renew
The triumph and have them decorate
The arch and stone again?
Surely those flowers are withered, the army
Now on a distant plain.

But some morning when you are washing up,
Or some afternoon, making a cup
Of tea, possibly you will see
The heavens opening and a lot
Of saints singing with bells ringing.
But then again, possibly not.

Published in *The Serpent* – Burgess/Wilson's first poem in print. Ascribed to F.X.
Enderby in *Inside Mr Enderby*, Part Three, Chapter One, section 2, where it takes
the form of a final, cryptic visitation by the Muse, who has abandoned Enderby and
left him suicidal. Burgess said (*LWBG*) that he had never quite understood the
poem himself: '...To me I suppose it was any young man rejecting the mother who
had produced and sustained him to the point of his finding an arrogant freedom.'
Tirzah, in Burgess's recollection, was an embodiment of the physically maternal
from the private mythology of William Blake: 'I do not propose checking on this.'

The Music of the Spheres

I have raised and poised a fiddle
    Which, will you lend it ears,
Will utter music's model:
    The music of the spheres.

By God, I think not Purcell
    Nor Arne could match my airs.
Perfect beyond rehearsal
    My music of the spheres.

Not that its virtue's vastness –
    The terror and drift of stars.
For subtlety and softness
    My music of the spheres.

The spheres that feed its working,
    Their melody swells and soars
On thinking of your marking
    My music of the spheres.

This musing and this fear's
Work of your maiden years.
Why shut longer your ears?
Look, how the live earth flowers!
The land speaks my intent:
Bear me accompaniment.

Said to have been written by F.X. Enderby at the age of 17, and published in *Inside Mr Enderby*, 1963. Reprinted, with minor variants, at the very end of the verse novel *Byrne*, dated to 'Ash Wednesday 1993' and published posthumously in 1995.

To Amaryllis after the Dance

Semitic violins, by the wailing wall
      Weep their threnody
For the buried jungle, the tangled lianas;
Or say that was before, in the first flush,
And say that now
A handful of coins, image and milled edge worn,
Is spilled abroad, and determines
Our trade of emotions. Over this background are imposed
Urges, whose precise nature it is hard
To etch out, to define.
(Shells, shaped by forgotten surges).
One never gets to know anything really, having no word
To body forth a thought, no axe
To reach flagged soil, no drills
To pierce to living wells. It would tax
My energies overmuch now to garner you
Out of worn coins, worn shells.

Published in *The Serpent* and signed 'J.B.W.'. Ascribed to F.X. Enderby in *Enderby Outside*, Part Two, Chapter Three, section 4, where it is identified as one of Enderby's juvenilia: he squirms and blusters as his muse-figure reads it to him with sardonic intent. There are a few substantial variants in the later version, including 'Gnash their threnody' for 'Weep their threnody' (l.2), 'difficult to define' for 'hard/To etch out' (l.10) and 'One understands so little, having no words' for 'One never gets to know anything really, having no word' (l.12), as well as some minor changes. The novel's mock-scholarly appendix identifies it as one of three early poems which 'cannot be traced either in published or manuscript form'.

Girl

She was all
Brittle crystal;
Her hands
Silver silk over steel;
Her hair harvested
Sheaves shed by summer;
Her grace in repose the flash
Of the flesh of a river swimmer.
That was not nature's good;
She nothing understands.
Horrible now she should
Use to her own ends.

Published in *The Serpent*; signed 'J.B.W.' Re-attributed, in fragmentary and re-written form (second person singular for third person singular: 'You are all'), to F.X. Enderby, as one of his juvenile productions, in *Inside Mr Enderby*, Part One, Chapter Two, Section 3.

Anciently the man who showed
Hate to this father with the sword
Was bundled into a coarse sack
With a screaming ape to claw his back
And the squawking talk of a parrot to mock
Time's terror of air-and-light's lack
Black
And the writhing litheness of a snake,
Then he was swirled into the sea.

But that was all balls and talk,
Nowadays we have changed all that,
Into a cleaner light to walk
And wipe that mire off on the mat.
So when I saw his end was near
My brain was freer
And scrawled a cancellation then
Of all the accidents of birth,
And I had a better right to the earth
And knew myself more of a man,
Shedding the last squamour of the old skin.

Written shortly after the death of Burgess/Wilson's father, Joseph Wilson (1883–1938). Ascribed, under the title 'Independence Day' and with a few significant variants ('creeping torpor' for line 8's 'writhing litheness', 'mind' for line 15's 'brain' and 'snapped its thumb and finger' for line 16's 'scrawled a cancellation'), to F.X. Enderby in *Enderby Outside*, Part Two, Chapter Three, Section 3. Enderby's new muse-figure reads it to him accusingly; he denies all knowledge of having written it, or of feeling any sense of animosity towards his father. See p. 21, 'Father of fire'.

September 1938

There arose those winning life between two wars,
Born out of one, doomed food for the other,
Floodroars ever in the ears.

Slothlovers hardly, hardly fighters:
Resentment spent against stone, long beaten out of
Mind, resigned to the new:
Useless to queue for respirators.

Also, what worse chaos to return to:
Home, limbs heavy with mud and work, to sleep
To sweep out a house days deep in dirt.

Knowing finally man would limbs, loin, face
Efface utterly, utterly, leave regal in his place
Engines rusting to world's end, heirs to warfare
Fonctionnant d'une manière automatique.

First published in *The Serpent;* signed 'J.B.W.'. Ascribed, with several variants, to F.X. Enderby in the Appendix to *Enderby Outside;* reclaimed, in a form closer to the original, in *LWBG*. The last line comes from Flaubert's *Un Coeur Simple*; the nightmare image of machines fighting each other is inspired by the popular British science-fiction film *Things to Come*, scripted by H.G. Wells.

Eden

History was not just what you learned that scorching day
Of ink and wood and sweat in the classroom, when mention
Of the Duke of Burgundy lost you in a voluptuous dream
Of thirst and Christmas, but that day was part of history.

There were other times, misunderstood by the family,
When you, at fifteen, on your summer evening bed
Believed there were ancient towns you might anciently visit.
There might be a neglected platform on some terminus

And a ticket bought when the clock was off its guard.
Oh, who can dismember the past? The boy on the friendly bed
Lay on the unpossessed mother, the bosom of history,
And is gathered to her at last. And tears I suppose

Still thirst for that reeking unwashed pillow,
That bed ingrained with all the dirt of the past,
The mess and lice and stupidity of the Golden Age,
But a mother and loving, ultimately Eden.

One looks for Eden in history, best left unvisited,
For the primal sin is always a present sin,
The thin hand held in the river which can never
Clean off the blood, and so remains bloodless.

And this very moment, this very word will be Eden,
As that boy was already, or is already, in Eden,
While the delicate filthy hand dabbles and dabbles
But leaves the river clean, heartbreakingly clean.

Ascribed to F.X. Enderby in the Appendix to *Enderby Outside*.

The Excursion

The blue of summer morning begs
The country journey to be made,
The sun that gilds the breakfast eggs
Illuminates the marmalade.

A cheque is smiling on the desk.
Remembered smells upon the lane
Breed hunger for the picaresque
To blood the buried springs again.

Here is the pub and here the church
And there our thirty miles of sun,
The river and the rod and the perch,
The noonday drinking just begun.

Let beer beneath the neighbour trees
Swill all that afternoon away,
And onions, crisp to sullen cheese,
Yield the sharp succulence of today.

Today remembers breaking out
The fire that burned the hayfield black.
An army that was grey with drought
Shows to my stick its fossil track.

Returning evening rose on rose
Or pomegranate rouge and ripe;
The lamp upon my pavement throws
The ectoplasm of my pipe.

Attributed to F.X. Enderby in the Appendix to *Enderby Outside*.

Summer 1940

Summer swamps the land, the sun imprisons us,
The pen slithers in the examinee's fingers,
And colliding lips of lovers slide on sweat
When, blind, they inherit their tactile world.

Spectacles mist, handveins show blue, the urge to undress
Breeds passion in unexpected places. Barrage balloons
Soar silver in silver ether. Lying on grass,
We watch them, docile monsters, unwind to the zenith.

Drops of that flood out of France, with mud and work
Stained, loll in the trams, drinking their cigarettes,
Their presence defiling the flannels and summer frocks,
The hunters to hound our safety, spoil the summer.

In *LWBG* – where the poem shows some minor variants ('Summer surprises, the sun imprisons us...' and so on) – Burgess reflects that the allusion to the Dunkirk evacuations dates the poem to early June. Re-ascribed to F.X. Enderby in the Appendix to *Enderby Outside*.

Spring in Camp 1941

War becomes time, and long logic
On buried premises; spring supervenes
With the circle as badge which, pun and profundity,
Vast, appears line and logical,
But, small, shows travel returning.
Circle is circle, proves nothing, makes nothing,
Swallows up process and end in no argument,
Brings new picture of old time.
Here in barracks is intake of birds,
The sun holds early his orderly room,
The pale company clerk is uneasy
As spring brings odour of other springs.
The truckdriver sings, free of the road,
The load of winter and war becomes
Embarrassing as a younger self.
Words disintegrate; war is words.

Written, according to *LWBG* (which gives the opening line as 'Time becomes war...'), in the following spring of 1942. Re-ascribed to F.X. Enderby in the Appendix to *Enderby Outside*, as one of his uncollected early poems.

Nymphs and satyrs, come away.
        Faunus, laughing from the hill,
Rips the blanket of the day
        From the paunch of dirty Will.

Each projector downs its snout,
        Truffling the blackened scene,
Till the *Wille's* lights gush out
        Vorstellungen on a screen.

Doxies blanch to silverwhite,
        All their trappings of the sport,
Lax and scattered, in this light,
        Merge and lock to smooth and taut.

See, the rockets shoot afar!
        Ah, the screen was tautest then.
Tragic the parabola
        When the sticks reel down again.

Written in the winter of 1942, when Wilson/Burgess was stationed at Eye in Suffolk. The *Wille* and *Vorstellungen* come from Schopenhauer, the 'parabola' from Spengler's *Decline of the West*: the heart attack which apparently kills off Enderby in the penultimate chapter of *The Clockwork Testament* is said to have the shape of a 'Spenglerian tragic parabola'. (*LWBG*'s version has 'Traffic the parabola' – presumably a misprint – and other less significant variants.) Re-ascribed to F.X. Enderby in *Inside Mr Enderby*, Part One, Chapter Four, section 3.

The Critic

Behold a prodigy – ballless born:
    Shielded so by a natural fence
    From the feared charge of impotence,
He laughs your little prick to scorn.

Written *c*. 1934.

Father of fire who, with bold simony,
      Didst steal the seed, cached high on Olympus,
Now in my need relive that felony
      And lean down to my praying, piteous.
      Be thou again as brave and bounteous
As when thou first didst bring that art of heat
      To nations bestial still and barbarous,
And fetch a match to light my cigarette.

Written *c.* 1938.

September 3, 1939

The night before last was Saturday night.
      The cinema crowds were excited.
The newsboys yelled 'Special!' with all their might,
Some said: 'It's going to be war all right!'
      The pimpled boys were delighted.

Yesterday morning, after mass,
      Chamberlain spoke on the wireless.
Jack Tollitt was screaming of poisoned gas:
'Seal all the windows!' And while I was
      Tired from the start, he was tireless.

And then I went quietly to my room,
      Avoiding stepmother, stepsister,
And in my head a cloud of gloom
Dripped dew on my individual doom
      And an endless nightmare vista.

I had never seen it so dark before:
      The streets had invisible craters.
Talk in the pub was about the war.
I drank until I thought no more
      Of democracy and dictators.

I drank until I thought no more
      Of Hitler's lust for dominion.
And so I said when a drink-soaked bore
Complacently turned and asked me for
      My own considered opinion:

'The king is only a cinema slide.
      The soldier puts cunt before country.
Last night two drunks were run over and died,
A neurotic attempted suicide,
      And a girl was raped in an entry.'

In *LWBG*, Burgess helpfully notes that 'The king is only a cinema slide' refers to the then-common practice of cinemas showing a still picture of the monarch at the end of the evening's screenings to prompt the audience to attention for the National Anthem; an 'entry' is a back alley.

Lines

For we were all caught in the shame of sleep.
Some of us rubbed an eye drowsily against the light; all were unprepared,
Webbed in its world and carrying phantom of a purpose:
Purpose of a phantom into waking, then waking, then knowing,
Then shame for such entry into day.
Forgive us untempered to the day.

Published in *The Serpent*; signed 'J.B.W.'.

What we made out of light
The light would not have.
So we hollowed out a grave
Where light has forever set.

Caught unawares in breach
Of fast or out of shrift,
Or what of festering speech
Upon the air was left.

As the spent hornblende numb
The eternity ever to come,
Over dead brains we bear
As we once bore the weight of the infinite air.

Published in *The Serpent*; signed 'J.B.W.'.

Well, my Eurydice, that was pain enough,
        Having only your name to call on in the night.
Both day and night were long enough.
        Now I lead you laboriously back to the light.

Hell played at forfeits. On a swivel of the head
        Rested your return. As one might stab a pin
Idly at a fly for its irrelevant end,
        The world was plunged in original sin.

That was not in the pattern of our lives,
        Whose miraculous fabric has for every strand
Accounted. Wantonly the destroyer unweaves,
        Just as he hides time's secret in his hand.

But it is true I should have been destined then,
        Climbing alone back to the light, to have met
The deserved logical end. The tree that has been
        Fruitful only stays to be fruitful yet.

The undergrowth of laws that sees no light –
        This I believe in as much as anything.
Hell would have seen you no Proserpina
        Nor sent you back to wither up the spring.

Written *c*. 1939. Published in *The Serpent*; this version revised *c*. 1986.

All the ore
        that, waiting, lay
for the later working
I melted before
its time
to make you ornaments for a day.
And all else, too
I drew out, there is no more.
For between man and man at the last
there rests at least shame.

Published in *The Serpent*; signed 'J.B.W.'.

A History

Anyway, there emerged from his mind's cellar
The forged stamp of the image of goddess,
And it fell upon her,
Almost, as it were, *per accidens*.
And with it a pitiful dual approach,
Half Shelley, half Flaubert.
He broached and broke the hymen of her lips
After three weeks' work, and was pre-occupied
By the technique, art for art's sake, of his kisses.
It was an attempt, having carved her pedestal,
To raise himself, almost by a metaphysical
Conceit, and to conduct love
On the level of Ideas, out of the clogs of time,
Seeing ethereal virtues in the bones
Of a paradigm.
O granted it was to become a grammar of love,
Yet who might construct that language, the vibrant speech
Sprung out of earth, from what had shed
All but archetypes, supposing the language dead?
Anyway, they reached complete intimacy,
And it was all on this level, carved out cleanly in time.
A fulfilling of all parts of the act, except
That it was playing from score, that a pattern was imposed,
That there was no growth out to become the pattern.
And he at least was amazed at the futility,
Thought the whole thing overrated; out of mind
Were the sweat and labour to compass an ecstasy.
But with her an unpurposed external heat
Had achieved the loosening of the icefloes. A late spring
Became a wonder in her. Her body began
To flower in its own right.
He saw that its opening to man
Was what he had done, that that was the accomplished fact
That had to be greater to her than their personal history,
The released woman more than the melted she.
Stricken, he escapes to the war.
In absence her image reverts to that of the goddess crystallised
About his longings; not before

Might she impartially have watched his spasm worked out
In her the instrument. But today
He is outside his handiwork, the unpremeditated lord
Of creation, and that one connecting cord
Shrivelled away.

Published in *The Serpent*; signed 'J.B.W.'.

Useless to hope to hold off
The unavoidable happening
With that frail barricade
Of week, day or hour
Which melts as it is made,
For time himself will bring
You in his high-powered car,
Rushing on to it,
Whether you will or not.

So, shaking hands with the grim
Satisfactory argument,
The consolation of bone
Resigned to the event,
Making a friend of him,
He, in an access of love,
Renders his narrow acres
Golden and wide enough.

And this last margin of leaving
Is sheltered from the rude
Indiscreet tugging of winds.
For parting, a point in time,
Cannot have magnitude
And cannot cast shadows about
The final kiss and final
Tight pressure of hands.

Written in Gibraltar, *c*. 1945. It won Wilson/Burgess the Governor's Poetry Prize.

Adderbury

Here ruined farmers, in new hacking-coats,
Pour Scotch and ram fat bacon down their throats;
And children, obdurately red and flaxen,
Proclaim the crass inbreeding of the Saxon.
Observe the maidens who, with brawny arms,
Gush the seductive fragrance of the farms.
They feel the body should be mainly meat,
That ankles have no function and that feet,
Disdaining shape and glorying in size,
Should shout a curious kinship to the thighs.
But lest with so much weight the streets should rock,
The dessicated matrons of good stock
(Though not for soup) tune their patrician reeds
In shops which specialise in tasteless tweeds,
Then hog the pavements with their barking spouses
Before they seek their deathwatch-rotting houses,
Where flies die in the port and rabbit, stewed,
Provides for dog and man a basic food.

… The manor gates are down, the past is dead.
American police patrol instead,
Save there, where feudalism's greasy scraps
Still touch the villagers who touch their caps
To soap king's lady or to upstart lord
Who licked the party's boots or swelled its hoard,
Trimming like mad or clinging like a louse
To be translated to the Upper House,
Whence now he comes to dogmatise and hector,
Sway the church sycophants and hound the rector.

Written in 1953; published in *LWBG*.

'Love water, love it with all your being,
But only from the well or the picnic spring.
Tasteless, but grateful in summer, embracing the hollow
Of any vessel. But never never follow
Water to the river or sea. Nor ever call
Master or Mistress Water in the bacchanal
Of public waters stirred up by the rough
Wind's rhetoric. Water from the well is enough.'

Attributed to the French rural poet 'Albert Ritaine' in the abandoned novel *It Is The Miller's Daughter*. Published in *Transatlantic Review*, 24 (Spring 1967), pp.5–15. Reproduced, with substantial variants (l.2: 'But only from the tap, never the spring'; ll. 5–8: '… never never call/On Master or Mistress Water in the fall/Of rivers or the sea churned by the rough/Winds' enmity. Water from the tap is enough.'), in *You've Had Your Time*, p.137.

The Sword

De Kalb, De Kalb, Flatbush Avenue: there, that bright March Saturday,
    I stood
With sclerotic toothache in kalb or calf, heavy on my cane,
A third leg, a British sword sheathed in cherrywood
For passive support, no tool or weapon. Wind, pain

Toothached in from East River. Well then, I thought, here you are,
Middleaged, claudicant, ignominiously propped
On a sheathed sword, wanting a cab, while car after car
Grinned by under the sun, Saturday gift for those who shopped.
                No cab stopped.

So I claudicated to the subway, wanting Brooklyn Heights (Clark),
But, instead of the Tunnel train, I caught the one for the Bridge:
Miles of metal and river and light, no expected comfortable dark
Fit for a middleaged Saturday with, at the end, the hermitage

Of the warm apartment and time to make myself seem younger
Or, at least, less middleaged and put that sword away,
At least for the evening. Canal (Centre). The cabless street, the hunger
To bury sword and myself out of the shameless Manhattan day

Increasing to worse toothache, though I am sure it was the wind
That mocked-up wet self-pity. More and more angrily I waved
The sword at the mocking full cabs. But then a sepia-skinned
Cabman responded and stopped. I entered, I was saved.

Back to Brooklyn. The driver, Alvin Lewis, found the street
And I found my key, but, to my incredulous shock,
The apartment door would not open. In bathrobe and flat wet feet,
The woman below came up: no good: something wrong with the lock.

So what could I do but do the rounds of the bars –
Harry's, the Golden Rose, Jed's Bar and Grill
And the nameless others? Martinis, cheap cigars,
The nameless others, underwater caves with the shrill

Radio the voice of up there, the TV images like divers
Looking in on this mouthing world, fish, drinking like fish,
Lonely men glass-twirling, making it last, and truck-drivers
Swilling one down, then away, and no matter how much I would wish

To clean off the middleage for the evening and her, I had to accept my dirt
And the dirty brown taste of my mouth, unanaesthetised
By the ice, my flat wet feet and limp wet shirt
And earwax in my oxters, and brain that was only surprised

Out of its boredom by each radio chime
Showing it was earlier than I'd thought it could possibly be.
But time, as we know, must in time get the better of time,
So time came for slurred and claudicant me

To know I might be late, and, as the lights came on all down the river,
Brandish that snugly latent sword at the cabs with lights
Until Jack Greenbaum contracted to deliver
The sclerosis and the cane and the gin of Brooklyn Heights

And, somewhere inside, me, not claudicant but palpitant now.
Hundred-and-tenth Street, the pay-off, the elevator,
Her door, she, in in quick with 'I can't allow,
I can't really, it won't do, you know it won't do.' And she: 'Later:

Time for that later. Be calm, be calm.' But I'd gotten into the way
Of thrusting that hidden steel, and I thrust, to protect her youth,
To protect me from her youth. She grasped, and it came away,
Sweetly, the cherrywood, and there, like attenuated truth,

The sword flashed. I said: 'It's only to lean on, to strengthen the cane.'
'Yes,' she said, 'yes.' It flashed, strong and straight. 'Well,' she said,
And she felt the edge, the point. I tried to sheathe it again,
But she said: 'Lay it there on the bed,

In the middle.' So there it lay,
Virtue's protector in the old courting custom. Still, it flashed. I washed off
     the day
And middleage. Clean and hungry, I breathed
More calmly now, and, while she brought food, I looked at it unsheathed,
At least it was unsheathed, at last it was unsheathed.

Published in *Transatlantic Review*, 23 (Winter 1966–7), pp.41–3.

Imagination is your true Apollo.
        In our translunar skulls the moon's small beer.
Fact's crippled fancy. Acts are slow to follow
        Words (small cheese, I meant – small *green* cheese). We're
        Too long beyond the moon. The moon's too near.

Bored with the merely possible, SF
        Spends trillions on each fresh galactic race
Yet shells out not one cent to make us deaf
        To the shrill signals from the silver face,
        Attuning us to tunes from deeper space.

Still, it was all romance, drawn up from wells;
        Or myth – an uncertain lantern in the air,
Or Prester John's balloon, the Christian hell's
        Chill annexe, or the huntress in her chair.
        Now Armstrong (Neil) and Aldrin (Ed) are there,

And Collins with his clucking mothercraft,
        Old Glory on the desecrated crust
Is all th'old glory that, alas, is left.
        So glory in, in your progressive lust,
        These heroes who sift silver for its dust.

Where the black gods deliciously prevail,
        You find cool tribes. Our hot entropic plan
Submits to seeing human order fail,
        Erects inhuman order where it can,
        And smiles and sighs at lunonautic man.

Published in the *New York Times*, 21 July 1969.

Lines

inspired by the controversy on the value or otherwise of Old English studies

Our Norman betters
Taught English letters
To bathe in the fresh
Warm springs of the south
So turn your backs on
Anglo–Saxon
The þ in the flesh,
The æ in the mouth.

Early 1970s? The names of the two Anglo–Saxon letters are 'thorn' and 'ash' respectively.

LONGER POEMS

O Lord, O Ford, God Help Us, Also You
A New Year's Message for 1975

Unhouse that calendar: her dates are done,
Her whorings over. Get another one,
Try to pretend a new year has begun.
The diary, blank, apes sinlessness. This is
The most pathetic of all fallacies –
The springs-eternal hope of a 'fresh start'
In the core of winter or, down under, heart
Of summer (the same season, after all:
Both lack the sharp élan of spring or fall,
So very and oppressively much *here*).
The church is realistic: its new year
Does not begin until Easter. New Year's Day
Is part of Christmas time, roughly halfway,
Marked by the Circumcision – snip and bless
And bow half-heartedly to cleanliness.
But we, who groan from drink or, showering, sing,
Believe the first of January can bring
Regeneration magically about
Both in our psyches and the world without.
On Jan 6, 10 – in other words, a bit
Later, we will, we vow, get down to it.
Nonsense – it can't be done: that's definite.
Spring brings the true new, nature's statements are
Simple enough: all change is circular.
The firm ascending straight progressive line
Is dream geometry, that's all. In fine,
This Nineteen-Seventy-five will see us still
Churning in Seventy-four's Satanic mill.
Has any twelvemonth fed us more with fear?
Was ever a more salutary year?
At least we're learning and no more pretend
That history moves to a Hegelian end.

Utopia spells Erewhon, the earth's
Resources are not infinite, a birth's
Another burden in a hungry world,
Man's gobbled up the soil and also hurled
His poisons in the water and the air,
Hell is a fact and no mere Sunday scare,
America as Eden's dead and gone,
The Devil rides, and so on and so on.
Men we thought big are now revealed as little,
Conniving and contriving, mean and brittle,
Power-hungry merely, greedier than us,
Vindictive, ignorant, pusillanimous,
Liars, vulgarians, and ugly too
(Truth's beauty, and the antithesis is true).
I gawped at New York television while
Your Ford, unflawed by an ironic smile,
Announced to the whole world: *Truth is a glue.*
O Lord, O Ford, God help us, also you.
Half a millenium has gone by since
Great Niccolò penned precepts for a Prince,
But in those unregenerate days at least
A prince, however hard he played the beast,
Saw statues hovering over him and read
Plato and Aristotle: the huge dead
Were still alive. But now, alas, it looks
As if the drughead's *Nothin', man, in books*
Infects the castles where our rulers sit
(*History*, that other Ford once said, *is s—t*).
The men that British rotten boroughs sent
To hector in a venal Parliament
Fulfilled no democratic precepts, yet
Saw that their own mean times were soundly set
In an unfolding swathe of destiny;
Man was, and had been, and would always be
What Homer, Seneca, Thucydides,
Xenophon, Cicero, and more like these
Had limned. They saw their legislative task
As somehow philosophical, would ask,
As Jefferson and Lincoln did, the one
Sound question: *What is man, what must be done*
By government, man's servant, to fulfil

The deeper longings of his higher will?
For politics was metaphysics, art,
Eloquence, knowledge of the human heart,
That is now sunk into a disrepute
Shameful and shameless, all too absolute.

This year will pose the question once again:
Where shall we go to seek superior men?
Superior in what? – a voice asks then:
The answer: In no more than being men.
The great technician's no superior man –
Only a larger type of artisan,
Extensive of his system or machine.
We need philosophers, not men who've been
Exalted through their skill at shyster's tricks,
Who shell out shibboleths, who fox, who fix,
Committed to the timocratic view
That wealth is power, and neither is for you.
Add wealth and power to vulgar ignorance,
And you can tune up for our *Totentanz*.
The worship of the base is here to stay:
I heard a British union leader say:
'They brought the plain men where they are today,
The great men: let them sleep, their task is done.'
Exactly. Let your son, and your son's son,
Inherit demo–ethics, demo–art,
And learn this demo–decalogue by heart:
First, order your instructors what to teach,
Since a man's grasp must not exceed his reach:
Spit on the higher values when you can,
Unsanctified by democratic man;
Permit free speech, though, since it can't effect
A blasting of the walls of the elect:
To slay – what is it but to put to sleep?
Computers cost much, human souls are cheap.
Lie all you wish, for who knows what truth is?
Play games among the ruined languages,
Jettison *why* and concentrate on *how*;
Assign a prime reality to *now*;
Deny responsibility for *then*;
Consume, and damn posterity – amen.

To opt out of this midden into dreams –
Communes or opiates – to many seems
The desperate one solution. I say: turn
Once more to the necessity to learn,
Not make a *tabula rasa* of your head,
But cram it with philosophy instead;
Leave inarticulacy to the loathed
Nude apes up there: let us at least be clothed,
Attack from knowledge and not just from rage:
Reject from reason. In another age,
Your fathers spoke thus, and did not the grey
Poet on Paumanok cry out: *Obey*
Little; resist much – let those four words be
A lasting slogan for the polity?
Love man the social animal, but hate,
On principle, the engine called the State;
Burn out the evil centre, and resolve
To flaunt a banner blazoned with *Devolve,*
Devolve. Then, last, remember Maynard Keynes:
People alone have virtue in their veins;
All goverments are evil. This he knew.

Comparatively, things go well for you,
America. I know – smog makes you cough,
Too many citizens are badly off
(Meaning, by Asian standards, millionaires),
The story of West 77th Street scares
The living daylights out of us – but still
Shocked citizens attempt to work their will
(Devolve, devolve) despite the apathy.
Your dreams, like ours, revolve on bankruptcy,
Moral or fiscal, both, inflation and
Entropy. Here, in Italy's sad land
(Gorgeous December sheens Bracciano's lake,
Clear as a bell beyond, my tired eyes take
Soracte in, that Horace used to know,
All candidly nival, tipped with snow),
Bankruptcy sits beside us, walks the streets,
Takes coffee in the café, chats and eats,
A trusted friend, who never lets you down.
Bankruptcy blows and petrifies the town,

Shuts the museums, spares the mailman's boots,
Blanks out the teevoo, clears the roads, recruits
Spray-gunning thugs who scrawl *Death* on the plinths,
Chokes up the bureaucratic labyrinths,
Hides oil and salt, makes impotent the laws,
But places truncheons in the policeman's paws.
Inflation? Ah, we beat all records here –
A 20 (minimal) % per year.
England, my country, mother of the free,
Is crammed with paper money too. You'll see
Financial columns crammed with reasons why:
The petromoney of the sheiks, the sly
Printing of empty paper by the State,
The blackmail of the unions, some great
Cryptoconspiracy all bloody red
That loves to strike and, striking, strikes us dead.
So England shivers, and the coal's undug,
Darkness abets the murder and the mug,
And light and heat assume definitive
Value – i.e., more than one has to give.
'The oil is Allah's,' yodels the bilal,
'Therefore the Peoples of the Scriptures shall
Learn who the Chosen People really are.'
So freezing people on a cooling star
Envy the Indians, who rarely freeze
But die instead from other maladies.
We're all in this – you there and we back here –
Seeing fresh millions added every year
To swell the hordes of those ordained to starve.
The rich man has a juicy joint to carve,
But no joint's big enough to palliate
The hunger of the hundreds at the gate.
Hinc illae lacrimae. A single penny
Is indivisible among the many,
So is a dime, a quarter, dollar – hence
We justify our modest affluence.

Courage! Though life is feeble, life persists
(Persists? Increases, cry the pessimists).
The Orinoco cannibal affirms:
Better for friends to eat you than the worms.

As you believe that men have reached the moon,
Believe that anthropophagy will soon
Solve all our problems, justifying war,
Since here's a noble cause to wage it for.
The fighting young, the flower of every land,
Will fall in battle and will then be canned.
Try this, the supermarkets will proclaim:
Munch MANCH or MONCH or MENSCH, or some such name.
Meawhile, although the demonstrator cries:
'Each time you laugh, another Indian dies,'
Let's greet old two-faced Janus with dry eyes.
'Whatever the year brings, it brings nothing new,'
Wrote Rose Macaulay. True – it was always true.
Walk on the sidewalk's edge, avoid the dark,
Watch out for pederasts in Central Park,
Read Plato and not *Playboy*, cease to try
To see life as a thing to quantify,
Cherish the gunman, guardian of the door,
And you'll come through. You came through '74.

Published in *The New York Times Magazine*, 29 December 1974. President Nixon,
threated with impeachment, had resigned his office on 9 August, and was succeeded
by his Vice-President, Gerald Ford.

Verses for the Seventieth Birthday
of Vladimir Nabokov

That nymphet's beauty lay less on her bones
Than in her name's proclaimed two allophones,
A boned veracity slow to be found
In all the channels of recorded sound.
Extrude an orange pip upon the track,
And it will be a pip played front or back,
But only in the kingdom of the shade
Can diaper run back and be repaid.
Such speculations salt my exile too,
One that I bear less stoically than you.
I look in sourly on my lemon trees,
Spiked by the Qs and Xs of Maltese,
And wonder: Is this home or where is home?
(Melita's caves, Calypso's honeycomb.)
I seek a clue or cue. Just opposite,
The grocer has a cat that loves to sit
Upon the scales. Respecting his repose,
One day he weighed him: just 2 rotolos.
In this palazzo wood decays and falls;
Buses knock stucco from the outer walls,
Slam shut the shutters. Coughing as they lurch,
They yet enclose the silence of a church,
Rock in baroque: Teresan spados stab
The Sacred Heart upon the driver's cab,
Whereon, in circus colours, one can read
That *Verbum Caro Factum Est*. Indeed,
I think the word is all the flesh I need –
The taste and not the vitamins of sense,
Whatever sense may be. I like the fence
Of black and white that keeps those bullocks in –
Crossboard or chesswood, Eurish gift of Finn –
The 'crossmess parzel'. If words are no more
Than *pyeoshki*, preordained to look before,
Save for their taking *chasse*, they alone,
And not the upper house, can claim a throne
(Exploded first the secular magazines
And puff of bishops). All aswarm with queens,

42

Potentially, that board. Well, there it is:
You help me counter the liquidities
With counters that are counties, countries. Best
To read it: *Caro Verbum Factus Est.*

Written in Malta, 1969.

Two allophones: see the opening of Humbert Humbert's narration in *Lolita*, which emphasises the two distinct allophones of the phoneme /1/ in her name.

Verbum Caro Factum Est: The Word was made Flesh.

Caro Verbum Factus Est: The Flesh was made Word. [But *caro* is feminine, so the line should perhaps be rewritten as: *Caro Verbum Facta Est.*]

Homage to Ogden Nash

I have never in my life said anything other than laudatory
Of the work of Ogden Nash, whose innovations were chiefly auditory,
Meaning that he brought a new kind of sound to our literary diversions
And didn't care much about breaking the poetic laws of the Medes and
    the Persians.
He uses lines, sometimes of considerable length, that are colloquial and
    prosy
And at the end presents you with a rhyme, like a twin-flowered posy
Or really, when you come to think of it, a pair of dwarf's gloves.
This bringing together of the informal and the formal is what his genius
    chiefly loves.
I am trying to imitate him here, but he is probably quite inimitable.
My own talent for this sort of thing being limited and his virtually illim-
    itable.
Moreover, he was American and I am incorrigibly British,
And the British, when writing light verse, tend to the facetious and
    skittish,
While he is dry, like a martini, and wittily New Yorkish,
Hardly ever sentimental or mawkish (this doesn't rhyme in American,
    which sounds its r's, so let me suggest oleaginous, like-the-fat-of-cold-
    porkish).
Not that he always writes like this: he can be brief and epigrammatical,
Allowing the long and formless line occasionally to enjoy a Sabbatical.
I suppose, when you come to think of it, he is like Alexander Pope,
Not of course in any way pontifical, he would not be such a dope,
But concerned with keeping his sense enclosed in a couplet, far from
    heroic,
Though the line is Epicureanly expansive, not stringently stoic.
I suppose, in a way, it's a marriage of Whitman and Dryden,
Since the latter taught verse to contract and the former permitted it to
    widen.
You can zigzag across the road but sometime or other you have to stop,
Because the rhyme tells you to, like a fairly amiable cop.
What kind of a writer is he – serious or jocular?
Is he democratically beerbarrelish or classically popular?
In the works of literary reference, where the serious have traditionally
    dominated,
You will not find Ogden Nash so much as nominated,

And he is virtually unknown to the aficionados of Harold or Denise
    Rob(b)ins:
He has not, in fact, been wound on to either of the two opposed bobbins.
Like William Schwenck Gilbert, another comic writer admitted to be
    sizeable,
He is, in the last analysis, pretty well uncategorisable.
Americans have learned from the music hall the importance of accurate
    timing
But from Gilbert the essential wittiness of unusual rhyming.
I say no more. In the face of the unanalysable I must not be analytical.
And when a writer is beyond criticism it is stupid to attempt to go all
    critical.
In a dictionary the term Ogden Nashish
Could only apply to Ogden Nash, who is as addictive as hashish
And ultimately unique, as Caruso or some other distinguished tenor is,
Or, if you wish it in Latin, *sui generis*.

Published as the 'Introduction' to Ogden Nash, *Candy is Dandy*.

Five Extracts from *Moses*

1. From Chapter One, *The Bondage*

Now there arose up a new king over Egypt,
Which knew not Joseph. And he said unto his people:
Behold, the people of the children of Israel
Are more and mightier than we.
The great intellectual eroded face of the Pharaoh,
The tired eroded voice, the wasted body in gold cloth,
The ringed claws grasping the sphinx arms
Of the pharaonic throne, aromatic gums asmoke,
Slaves with feather fans, effigies, effigies,
All empty-eyed. The councillors listened.
'Their men are bursting with seed. Their women
Are round like fruit. Their encampments are loud
With the bleating of children. They multiply, multiply.'
A councillor said: 'Your divine majesty
Has some immediate danger in mind?' And Pharaoh:
'War. Should there be war
With some alien people, might not these
Aliens in our midst join with our enemies?
Immediate danger. Let danger be always immediate.
It is a sound thesis. Let us defend ourselves
Before we are attacked.' And another councillor:
'Your divine majesty's immediate orders?'
'I specify nothing,' Pharaoh said. 'I say:
Deal wisely with them. Use – immediate wisdom.'
So immediate wisdom, in the dust of hooves
And the shine of metal, thundered into the sheep-shearing...

2. [Marching song of Pharaoh's soldiers]

Here's the way
We earn our pay
Who's the enemy we slay?
Baby Israelites if they
Have balls between their legs.

That's no way
To earn your pay
We would rather any day
Take their mothers and then lay
Our balls between their legs.

3. From Chapter Eleven, *The Golden Calf*

[*While Moses is away conferring with the Almighty on Horeb, the Israelites lapse into pagan brutality and orgies, worshipping a Golden Calf. We encounter them in the middle of a hideous scene.*]

             ...Dancing, rutting,
The disrobing of a screaming boy by men who
Slavered in lust. Lust, drunken fighting,
And Dathan, drunk, screaming ecstatic: 'There has to be
A sacrifice, the god wants a sacrifice,' pointing
Among cheers and growls to a trembling girl. Miriam
Stood in Aaron's place, hardly heard: 'Cannot you
Understand? This is another kind of
Slavery. God, the true God, sees all and will punish
Terribly. Turn away from your sin before it is
Too late.' A cloud covered the thin moon,
And some, in slow fear, looked up. 'A sign,' she cried.
Then the cloud passed. 'Cease your wickedness.
God will forgive, God will understand.' But they
Dragged her down, stripping and beating her, lifting
The battered dull gold effigy to its old place,
Holding the terrified naked girl beneath
On a jagged slab, while a hulking lout as priest
Prayed gibberish to the calf – *O guk O guk*
Bondage of unintelligibubble. Gaaaaaar!

And he raised the knife and plunged, plunged
Till he was tired of plunging. Horror, awe,
Joy. He covered his arms and head with blood,
He daubed the loins of the calf in it, and now
The crowd surged about, dipping in blood,
Anointing their own loins. They brought a boy,
Already stunned with a sharp rock, and rent him,
And some drank the blood and chewed and spat out
The rent flesh. (A drunk made slobbering love
To a woman equally drunk, and, equally drunk,
Another man wrestled with him in jealousy
And then took a stone and spilled his brains.
All brains and blood about them, he and she
Made slobbering love.) The dull gold effigy
Was everywhere daubed with blood and brains and seed
And, like red seed, blood dripped from its loins.
Battered and sobbing, Miriam crawled to her tent
And found Eliseba there, and the children, safe,
But where was Zipporah? The moon was setting.
The faintest dawn-streak flushed. And high on Horeb
Moses emerged from the cloud, under his arms
Two tablets, intricately carved, grim, growing gentle
As he bade the sleeping Joshua awake.
Joshua looked up, saw the tablets, saw
A kind of white light about the head of Moses,
And, seeing, knelt. 'Rise, Joshua,' he was told.
'We have mischief below. We must go down to the mischief.'
So they descended as dawn grew, till at length,
From a ridge above the encampment, they saw enough:
A beast of metal drunkenly on a plinth,
Daubed with dried blood, some of it flaking off,
A naked body, too mauled to show its sex,
Men and women sleeping naked, corpses,
Blood everywhere, odd whimpering cries
From sources unseen, a half-devoured whole sheep,
The flies already at their work, shattered wine jugs,
Blood. 'Call,' said Moses quietly. 'Call, Joshua.'
So Joshua put his hollowed hands to his cheeks
And called a long sound. He called and called.
Some stirred, then slept again, moaning. Some
Stirred and listened and wondered, dazed, then saw

Dried blood in the sun. Miriam heard,
Ceasing to sob, and Aaron, bruised, dry blood on him,
Heard. Many heard, looking up in fear, and wonder,
Seeing bones, spilt wine, soon silent in the camp,
Two men walking. Zipporah, lying alone,
Blood on her garment, saw: light from his head,
His, shining, and behind his head an instant
The battered horns. He did not seem to see her.
Then Aaron stood before Moses, saying nothing,
Having nothing to say, then fell down in tears,
And Moses said, in sadness: 'Not enough knowledge.
Never enough. And out of ignorance, evil.
The work wasted. All the work wasted.'
In his arms were the stones, painfully chiseled.
'The covenant is broken. We must start again.'...

4. From Chapter Sixteen, *Zimri*

[*Acting on Moses's direct orders, the supposedly incorruptible Zimri recces the streets of decadent Moab.*]

Zimri in night town, walking amid torches,
Music, dance, passed a man and a woman
Embracing naked and frankly in the shadows.
He shuddered, then grew angry when he observed
An Israelite he knew – Gaddiel, son of Sodi?
Mounting steps to a temple, or what seemed to be
A temple, its front carved with contorted bodies
In acts of love unknown to the Israelites.
He followed but had already lost him in the shadows
When he entered a chamber leading off the porch of the temple,
Lighted by torches and spitting oil lamps, gross
With pagan effigies. His heart thumped, he looked about him,
And then a woman emerged from the shadows, a Moabite,
In garments he took for those of a priestess, ugly,
Obscenely so, appallingly, seductively so.
She spoke honey: 'You, sir, are a stranger –'
'An Israelite,' he answered, his voice not
Well in control, and she said: 'Ah, a follower
Of the new god we are hearing so much about.

The god of vengeance which is called justice.' He:
'A God of love, we are taught. Of love. A God.'
But she said, smiling: 'So – not a new god, then.
You are interested, stranger, in our faith?'
Stiffly he said: 'My own faith is enough
To keep my organ of faith fully occupied.
Other faiths are an abomination, so we are taught.
Many gods – all of them unclean:
The way of the Moabites, we are taught, much like
The way of the accursed Egyptians.' She said:
'The Egyptian gods are gods of death – so *we* are taught.'
He said: 'Madam, you have been well instructed.
I must tell you that I am here offically.
Are Israelites frequenting this temple? I thought I saw
One enter now.' She said: 'Israelites, Moabites –
The names mean nothing. Servants of Ba'al
Come to the temple to worship. I do not inquire
Beyond the faith, beyond the willingness
To embrace the faith.' – 'And what,' he said, 'is the faith?'
She said to him softly: 'Look about you.' He looked
At effigies, paintings, showing modes of love
Not known to Israel, she talking the while,
Holding a torch to light the effigies:
'The faith is love, but not perhaps love
As a desert people will know it. You desert folk
Live in wide space and feel a desire to fill it.
You are a nation, so I hear, that is desirous
Of being great among the peoples of the earth.
You breed, you fill your tents with children. With you
The coupling of man and woman is to that end.
You do not talk or dream of the ecstasy of love –
Only the seed's flow, the setting of the seed to work.
To you, the act of the man and woman is like the
Sowing of a field. To us, it is not so.'
Zimri gulped at some of the effigies.
'Whatever it is, this love of yours, it is an
Abomination before the Lord.' – 'Which Lord?' she asked.
Zimri said: 'There is only one – our God,
The creator and sustainer of the world,
The God of Israel, the God of mankind.'
She smiled. 'The God of a madman on a donkey –

That is how he appears to the Moabites.
But you must see what we mean by love. Come with me.'
He cried out: 'No. Blasphemy. Filth.' She said:
'It is blasphemy and filth to know that ecstasy
Which divides men from the beasts of the field? It is
Blasphemy and filth to know oneself
In the very living presence of the god?
The ecstasy is sent by the god: it is blasphemy
To reject it. The cleanness of the spirit,
From which all earthly dross is purged away –
To reject that is the sin of wallowing
In the filth of animals.' But Zimri cried: 'No. No.'
But he suffered himself, saying *no no* the while,
To be led to the inner temple, drawn there
In his own despite...

5. From Chapter Eighteen, *Jordan*

[*The last days of Moses.*]

And Moses said: 'Beloved, keep the commandments.
Love justice and mercy. Love the Lord our God,
For his ways are the ways of justice and mercy.'
And he saw that the time was coming for his people
To pass over the river and take up their inheritance.
So he bade the whole of the Israelite nation kneel,
And they knelt, and then he blessed them, saying:
'Happy art thou, O Israel. Who is like unto thee,
O people saved by the Lord, the shield of thy help
And the sword of thy excellency. There is none like unto your God,
Who rides upon the heavens. The eternal God
Is your refuge, and underneath are the everlasting arms.' Then the
    Israelite army
Saluted his greatness with shouts and with the clamour
Of drums and silver trumpets. So he moved
To the mountain, and Caleb and Joshua tried to help him
In his climb to its summit, but he waved their help aside.
He climbed and they watched him, thinking: *Strong as an ox,
With the eyes of an eagle*, but it was not true,
Not true any longer. The Israelites, shielding their sight

Against the sun, watched him long and long
Till he reached the top of the mountain. There he rested.
And after a time of rest he heard a voice,
His own voice, young again, saying unto him:
'Now, Moses, I will show you their inheritance.'
He said: 'But not mine,' with his old boldness,
The boldness of a prince. 'You are a hard
And unforgiving God.' The voice said, 'Unforgiving?
If you but knew, if you only knew. But I
Have sworn and made my covenant with man.
I shall not again destroy him for his sins.
Yet I shall torment him with dissatisfaction,
For only in me shall he be satisfied.
Look now – all the land of Gilead, unto Dan.'
And Moses stood to look, seeing the river,
And all the lands beyond the river, fair,
Rich and fair. 'Look. And all Naphtali
And the land of Ephraim and Manasseh,
And the land of Judah, unto the utmost sea.
And the plain of the valley of Jericho, city of palm trees,
Unto Zoar. This is the land which I swore
Unto Abraham, and Isaac, and unto Jacob,
Saying: I will give it unto thy seed.
Moses, I have caused thee to see it with thine eyes,
But thou shalt not go thither.' Moses did not
Weep, but he said again, with a princely boldness:
'You are a hard and unforgiving God – '
'Go down now. Return to the valley of Moab,'
Said the voice. And Moses said: 'To die.'
And the voice said: 'What else?' So he went down
And waited, willing death, which was not long,
For when a man's work is done there is only death...

Published 1976.

TRANSLATIONS AND ADAPTATIONS

The Eve of Saint Venus: from the Pervigilium Veneris

Tomorrow will be love for the loveless, and for the lover love.
The day of the primal marriage, the copulation
Of the irreducible particles; the day when Venus
Sprang fully-armed from the wedding blossoms of spray
And the green dance of the surge, while the flying horses
Neighed and whinnied about her, the monstrous conches
Blasted their intolerable joy.

Tomorrow will be love for the loveless, and for the lover love.
The swans, with garrulous throats, crash through the pools
In a blare of brass; the girl that Tereus
Forced to his will complains endlessly
Among the poplars, desperately forcing
The heartbreak message through, but only forcing
More and more ironic sweetness till
The ear faints with excess of sweetness.

Tomorrow shall be love for the loveless, and for the lover love.
The scrubbing and dusting, the worry about what to eat,
The stretched elastic of wages and housekeeping money
Ready to snap, the vertigo vista of debt
Shall no longer seem important; the housewife's fingers
Shall lose their creases of grime; the husband's hair,
Receding, will give him a look of Shakespeare. Honey
Will flow from the lips that meet in perfunctory greeting;
The good-night kiss will suddenly open a door,
And sleep then will be a bouquet with lights and music.

Tomorrow shall be luck for the luckless, and for the lucky luck.
The luckless punter will have unbelievable luck
And the bookmaker doubt his vocation. Houses will echo
With a fabulous smell of frying onions, steaks
Will be featherbeds of salivating thickness.
Beer will bite like a lover and prolong its caress
Like cool arms in a hot bed. And clocks
Shall, in the headlong minute before closing-time,
Not swoop to the kill, but hover indefinitely,
Like beneficent hawks.

Tomorrow shall be love for the loveless, and for the lover love.
The bed will be no monster's labyrinth,
But spirals winding to a blinding apex,
Sharp as a needle, where the last shred of self
Is peeled off painlessly, and space and time are bullied
Into carrying their own burdens.

Tomorrow shall be love for the loveless, and for the lover love.
The map of love, spread on our knees, disclosing
The miraculous journey, shall not terrify
With lack of compass-points, with monstrous patches
Of *terra incognita*. Every sea-lane
Leads us home to each other, and always home
Is a new continent, of inconceivable richness.

Tomorrow shall be love...

Adapted from the anonymous Latin of the *Pervigilium Veneris*: 'Cras amet qui numquam amavit...'. Translated in 1952 as part of the short novel *The Eve of Saint Venus*, eventually published in 1964.

Ten Sonnets from the Roman Dialect of Giuseppe Gioacchino Belli

I

THE CREATION OF THE WORLD

One day the bakers God & Son set to
And baked, to show their pasta-maker's skill,
This loaf the world, though the odd imbecile
Swears it's a melon, and the thing just grew.
They made a sun, a moon, a green and blue
Atlas, chucked stars like money from a till,
Set birds high, beasts low, fishes lower still,
Planted their plants, then yawned: 'Aye, that'll do.'

No, wait. The old man baked two bits of bread
Called Folk – I quite forgot to mention it –
So he could shout: 'Don't bite that round ripe red
Pie-filling there.' Of course, the buggers bit.
Though mad at them, he turned on us instead
And said: 'Posterity, you're in the shit.'

THE EARTHLY PARADISE OF THE BEASTS
[a.k.a. THE BEASTLY PARADISE]

Animals led a sort of landlord's life
And did not give a fuck for anyone
Till man fucked up their social union
With gun and trap and farm and butcher's knife.
Freedom was frolic, roughish fun was rife,
And as for talk, they just went on and on,
Yakking as good as any dean or don,
While Adam stood there dumb, with a dumb wife.

This was the boss who came to teach them what
Was what, with harness, hatchet, stick and shot,
Bashing them to red gravy, thick and hot.
He stole their speech too, making sure he'd got
Dumb servitude – the plough; if not, the pot.
He had the last word. Nay, he had the lot.

PRIDE BEFORE A FALL
[a.k.a. ADAM]

If God made man, we've no call to regret
Man's love of blood and lack of bloody sense.
God, who's all what they call omnipotence,
Meaning he'll piss the bed and prove it's sweat,
Pissed on some clay and sweated cobs to get
A statue from it, sparing no expense.
Then he took breath and blew – *Haaaa Hadam.* Hence
Man's sometimes called the Puffed Up Marionette.

In just one minute he could spout out history
And write and read great tomes as tough as Plato's.
He knew it all when first he tottered bedwards.
The names of beasts and birds – no bloody mystery.
Like a greengrocer sorting out potatoes:
'This lot is whiteboys and these here King Edwards.'

BACK TO THE ROOTS
[a.k.a. ORIGINS]

A sort of interlude. Let's look at dogs.
At mastiff, Great Dane, greyhound, poodle, beagle,
The sausage hound, that yelps like a sick seagull,
Asthmatic bullpups honking hard as hogs.
Now men. Irish in bogs and Dutch in clogs,
Swarthy as turds, sharp-conked as any eagle,
The Jew and Turk. Then, trying to look regal,
Tea-slurping English, and French eating frogs.

Compare some doggy that leaps on to laps
With a prize wolfhound. Different as cheese and chalk.
In spite of this, our parish ballocks yaps
About us springing from a single stalk:
One primal bitch for pups, and one for chaps.
Did you ever hear such stupid fucking talk?

MAN
[a.k.a. MAN THE TYRANT]

This furred and feathered boss of bird and brute
Assumed the god, all bloody airs and graces,
Nor deigned to look down in his subjects' faces.
Treating each creature like a mildewed boot.
He swilled, he gorged, but his preferred pursuit
Mixed sticking pigs and whipping hounds on chases,
Marches through arches, blown brass and tossed maces,
With decking Eve, that bitch, in hunter's loot.

The beasts had hunted looks, being forced to make,
Poor wretches, the bad best of a bad job
And put up with that swine – all save the snake
Who, spitting like a kettle on a hob,
Weaved at the foul shapes tyranny can take
And hissed: 'I'll get you yet, you fucking snob.'

First published in *Malahat Review*, 44, October 1977. Revised versions in *ABBA ABBA* (1977)

II On Christ's Nativity

1. [ANNUNCIATION]

You know the day, the month, even the year.
While Mary ate her noonday bowl of soup,
The Angel Gabriel, like a heaven-hurled hoop,
Was bowling towards her through the atmosphere.
He crashed a window. Mary, without fear,
Saw him come through the hole in one swift swoop.
A lily in his fist, his wings adroop,
'Ave,' he said, and after that, 'Maria.

'Rejoice, because the Lord's eternal love
Has made you pregnant – not by orthodox
Methods, of course. The Pentecostal dove
Came silently and nested in your box.'
'A hen?' she blushed. 'For I know nothing of –'
The angel nodded, knowing she meant cocks.

2. [ENTER JOSEPH]

Only a few weeks after did our Virgin see
The need to make a matrimonial match,
To build a nest wherein the egg could hatch
(Her little belly had begun to burgeon, see).
It was therefore a matter of some urgency.
She didn't seek the freshest of the batch;
The one she gave her hand to was no catch,
But any port will do in an emergency.

The foolish gossips gossiped at the feast:
'She might have got a younger one, at least,
Not an old dribbler frosty in the blood.'
But that old dribbler standing by the side
Of such a beautiful and youthful bride,
Found his dry stalk was bursting into bud.

3. [THE VISIT]

Mary received, while burning Joseph's toast,
A letter. 'Who the hell – ?' (under her breath.
Aloud:) 'It's cousin Saint Elizabeth.
Elizabeth, it seemed, could also boast
A pregnancy, though not from the Holy Ghost.
Still, her next birthday was her sixtieth.
Though travel then was slow expensive death,
'We're coming,' Mary wrote, then caught the post.

They went. After a short magnificat,
The women were soon chattering away
Of cravings, morning sickness, and all that.
Joseph decided that he'd like to stay
A month or so, and so hung up his hat.
Better than sawing wood all bloody day.

4. [CIRCUMCISION]

Our Lady had a painful Christmas Day
And heaven the monopoly of mirth.
Between an ox and ass she brought to birth
A stableboy that stank of rags and hay.
His substitutive dad had to obey
The Law, so took the yelling lord of earth
Templewards, to have half a farthingworth
Of hypostatic foreskin cut away.

Thirty years later saw the blessed Lord on
A journey to the rolling river Jordan
To be baptised by Mary's cousin's son.
A Christian man thus sprang from a prepuceless
Jew. I call most turncoats fucking useless
But make a rare exception for this one.

5. [THE SLAUGHTER OF THE INNOCENTS 2]

King Herod now, to minimal applause,
Ordered the babies to be stuck like swine.
There was an uproar then in Palestine
And not, O Jesus help us, without cause.
Those who had seen this coming did not pause
To hide their babes, but let them croon or whine
As visible as laundry on the line,
While they had masses said to Santa Claus.

Their saviour (saviour?), halfway to the delta,
Smelt nothing of the filthy bloody welter
Nor heard the parents roar or ululate.
The troops of Herod smote and did not spare
But with each blow a splinter sought the air
And feebly knocked on heaven's heavy gate.

Times Literary Supplement, 23 January 1976. Revised versions in *ABBA ABBA*.

DRAMATIC VERSE, LIBRETTI AND LYRICS FOR MUSICALS

From Bizet's *Carmen*

Extracts from Carmen *(1986); An Opera in Four Acts by Georges Bizet; Libretto by H. Meilhac and L. Halevy, based on the story by Prosper Merimée.*

Act One

[*Enter Carmen*]

TENORS   Oh why
Won't you listen and deign to reply?
Oh why
Not a word or a blink of the eye?
Reply to the sigh that we're sighing again –
When will you give your love?
Won't you tell us when?

CARMEN   That old question again –
That *when?* How can I tell?
Tomorrow at ten.
Or never, no way.
But mark one thing well –
Not today!

[*She sings a habanera*]

Love's a beast that you'll never tame –
He's up the hills and then he's far away.
He won't come when you call his name,
But throw him out and he'll want to stay.

Give me gold in a silver sack
And I won't drop you a single stitch.
Stare right through me then turn your back
And see me fawn like a mongrel bitch.

It's love – sweet love –
Dear love – it's love.

For love's a gypsy through and through,
And law and logic he can live without.
If you'll love me, I won't love you,
But if I do then you had best watch out.

CHORUS   You'd best watch out!

CARMEN   If you love me, my love is something you must do without.

CHORUS   And so watch out!

CARMEN   If you don't love me,
            Then I'll teach you what love's all about.

            Love's a whirlwind and love's a fire
            And love's a landscape of summer snow.
            Seek out love in your best attire,
            And love will strip you and lay you low.

            Take this jewel and guard it well
            Then see it melt into scum and spit.
            Rail at love as a fiend from hell,
            And love will show you where the angels sit.

            For love's a gypsy through and through,
            And law and logic he can live without.
            If you'll love me, I won't love you,
            But if you do then you had best watch out.

CHORUS   You'd best watch out!

CARMEN   If I love you, your very manhood will be called in doubt.

CHORUS   And so watch out!

CARMEN   And love will tell you
              What the living hell it's all about!

*

CARMEN   Under the walls of Sevilla
              Stands Lillas Pastia's tavern,
              Where folk dance the gay seguedilla
              And drink manzanilla
              In a kind of candelabra'd cavern.
              There's pleasure to discover there,
              But I don't like it on my own.
              I'd rather take a lover there:
              A lady shouldn't drink alone.
              The one I had – the devil screw him
              And chew his carcase to the bone.
              Now my pour soul
              Needs some new wooing
              My heart is whole
              But empty as air.
              Though I've a dozen others queueing,
              They know there's nothing doing there.
              The week is over and I'm free from care:
              Who'd like some love? I've some to spare.
              My heart in hiding
              Longed for a new love,
              Then you came striding
              Into my view. Love,
              Make up your mind while you're able,
              There's a table laid for two
              Under the walls of Sevilla,
              Where we will swill manzanilla,
              And gypsy musicians
              Will strike up a rhythm for dancing to –
              So I'd like to go and frolic there with you!

My heart in hiding: Carmen is unconsciously echoing Gerard Manley Hopkins's *The Windhover*: 'My heart in hiding/Stirred for a bird…'

Act Two

[In Lillas Pastia's tavern. Carmen and her friends Mercedes and Frasquita perform a lively gypsy dance for the officers and their girls.]

MERCEDES The spanking of the tambourines,
The jingling of the rings of metal,
Makes any gypsy show her fettle,
For she knows what our gypsy music means.
Then add the clanging of guitars,
The magic of those supple fingers,
The buzzing of the strings that lingers
In a wonderful blur –
It's what I prefer
To any other sound beneath the stars.

La la la la, *etc.*

FRASQUITA And then we hear the stamping feet,
The earrings and the silver bangles
That comment on the jingle jangles
Of the music's loud and lusty beat.
The dancing and the song are wed.
As shy as any groom and bride,
They learn to set their fears aside
And they closely embrace,
And their bodies enlace
Upon a crimson-rose-empetalled bed.

La la la la, *etc.*

CARMEN Now dance and music are a flame –
They flaunt themselves like any harlot
In skirts of saffron, rose and scarlet –
They're the colours of joy and not of shame.
A whirlwind's blowing from the west,
A fever's rising in my breast,
The colour, noise and hellish quickness
Burn in my seething soul like a sickness!
Dance – and let the devil take the rest!

La la la la, *etc.*

CHORUS   He's here! Long live our torero!
                He's here! Long live our torero!
                Success! Long live Escamillo!
                Success! Long live Escamillo!
                Success! Success! Viva!

ESCAMILLO   Thank you all!
                And I can best respond
                By toasting what I call
                A kind of common bond.
                Vessels of beauty,
                Servants of duty –
                Danger is the only thing
                Of which we can be fond.
                When I stand
                And sniff the plaza's blood and sand
                And hear the eager crowd on every hand
                (Proof of their bliss is
                Bloodthirsty kisses)
                Then I know the way I go is where my destiny planned.
                Just before we start
                The feast of courage
                In a beating heart,
                I hear one voice apart,
                Speaking low of a reward that's waiting
                After all this gory show –
                So go, so go, so go
                To glory!

                Toreador,
                The flag of battle flies.
                Gird up your youth –
                Fame is the prize.
                Should fear besmear the dagger-point of truth,
                Take that chance in your stride.
                Remember, two dark eyes
                Look on with pride,
                And love is by your side.

What is this
That reeks of sudden death
And makes the people hiss
As they drew in their breath?
Stamping and lunging,
Heaving and plunging,
Snorting with his cup of anger full,
Here comes the bull!
For a start,
With a vindictive roar,
He tears a horse apart
And gores a picador.
Blind to this sorrow,
'Ah, bravo toro!'
Cries the cruel crowd that smells fresh blood
And yells for some more.
Bandilleros pierce the monster's hide.
He snorts with rage. He leaps.
He roars with wounded pride.
All but I rush to the arena's side.
While I hear that inner voice:
Rejoice,
You'll win,
Go in to glory!

Toreador,
The flag of battle flies.
Gird up your youth –
Fame is the prize.
Should fear besmear the dagger-point of truth,
Take that chance in your stride.
Remember, two dark eyes
Look on with pride,
And love is by your side.

Act Three

MICAELA   Why plead
For the thing I need –
Just a comforting arm
That will hold me from harm –
When he
Alone who could give it to me
Is grown cruel and strange
And is wedded to danger?
Most of the tales that we hear
Tell of one who was dear
But now has joined the lost.
Every day I pray:
God give him grace,
But God is not near
Or hides his face.

I'm afraid of one I daren't name.
Her very name conjures all ill.
She has chained his soul to her will
And made him leave the road of honour.
Her beauty is no gift of heaven.
Beautiful angels sinned and fell.
I know it's a weapon out of hell.
I fear the foul strength of her spell,
Still –
I'll lay the curses of the saints upon her,
And God will wish them well.

Yet guide my way,
God of good,
As I stray
Through this dark wood.
No stranger way
Feet have trod.
Comfort and stay me,
Dear God.

Act Four

[*The chorus of spectators acclaims the killing of a bull*]

CHORUS   See – that eye's
Ferocity dims. On
Sand he lies
His blood makes crimson.
Into his hide now
Steel's going to slide now.
So now – he goes – so now –
How fearful
The moment of truth –
The brutal bull
Meets courage and youth,
Also skill –
How clean is the kill!
The kill! The kill! The kill!
Victoria!
....

See – that eye's
Ferocity dims. On
Sand he lies
His blood makes crimson.
See the blood pour,
Gloriously gory.
He's gone – it's done – he's dead.
Take his corpse and hack it afresh
And tell the poor to gorge on his flesh.
....

Toreador, your battle has been won.
See where he lies –
Dead in the sun.
How skilfully you pierced the monster's hide,
With what anguish he died.
And now those two dark eyes
Award your prize –
The kiss of pride!

68

From Weber's *Oberon*

From Oberon, *a 'romantic and fairy opera in three acts', music by Carl Maria von Weber, original libretto by J.R. Planché (1856); freely adapted and updated from Planché in 1985.*

Act Two

[*No. 13: Rezia – an amateur opera singer, and former secretary in a Western embassy to a hostile Islamic state – has been taken hostage by the fiendish Ayatollah Harun and eventually rescued by her lover Hugh. The couple are shipwrecked in a a sudden storm. Left alone on a beach while Hugh seeks help, she recalls a favourite aria that seems to suit her current plight; it just happens to be the famous concert piece from* Oberon, *'Ocean! Thou mighty monster…'*]

REZIA   Ocean, you mighty monster,
            You are curled
            Like some green snake
            Around the living world.
            Dangerous enough when resting from the gale,
            A playground for the dolphin and the whale.
            But when you rear and hiss and strike as now,
            And gnaw the labouring ship from stern to bow,
            Chewing the mainmast and the garboard strake,
            Then, dragon sea, like you we cry and quake.
            Green and black, snowy, lacy-fleeced,
            Heaves in arms the heavy beast,
            Grendel seeks his fleshy feast.
            Shoreside bell, knell. Dear ones, weep now.
            Ocean's victims greenly sleep now.

            But see – I see the sea grow calmer –
            Hangman loosening the noose,
            Soldier taking off his armour.
            He declares, though grudgingly, a truce.
            Let the beating pulse grow limper,
            Let the clouds dissolve to fog,
            And the gale become a whimper,
            As of a fireside-dreaming dog.

The sun breaks weal but warm,
The sea's a jeweller's shop.
Like time itself, each storm
Must have a stop.

Sunset melts the cloudy webbing,
And the breezes moan in pity
As I see the lifeblood ebbing
From a bombed and blazing city.

This may be the last occasion
I shall be the witness of
Sea and sun and joy's invasion
At all blessings from above,
And be blessed with faultless love.

But there's something on the sea,
Something cream-and-silver shining.
It's a dolphin or, maybe,
Killer shark that's finished dining.

No, I see it now – a boat!
Yes – new-rinsed and bright – a sail.
Whose buoyant skill has kept afloat
Such a prey to the gale?

We're safe at last.
Oh, Hugh, where are you?
All our troubles are done, all buried in the past.
Make haste, gallant mast,
To us who were cast
On a friendless coast without a hope in view!

Quick – quick – give a sign now –
This scarf, this foulard, will do fine now.
They've seen me and answer this signal of mine.
Hurry, hurry, Hugh love.
Run now, run now, run now, run now,
Hugh my love!

With the gliding of a dancer
On the floor of a ballroom,
It is riding like a lancer,

Though this shore gives them small room
For their lay to.
They too smile!
Dearest, we will be home in a while.

With the gliding of a dancer
On the floor of a ballroom
It is riding like a lancer
With the answer
To all the rumours whispered by despair
That made us share a living hell.
All is well –
I can tell.

[*Alas, all is not well*]

[*From No. 14: Act Two Finale. While the human characters sleep, the fairies Oberon and Puck survey the moon-lit ocean, and watch the revels of its assorted denizens.*]

MERMAID 1   Life is good in my watery bed
Where I brood on life in the world overhead.
How do they breath in that razorsharp air?
What do they eat? There's no plankton floating up there.
Sometimes I soar to the roof of our world,
Head under that water that's mother-of-pearled.
Pearl up there, are you king of the sky?
Where is the shell of the oyster that taught you to fly?

MERMAID 2   Now and then I can see up aloft
A small flying fish with a buzzing so soft
The stars in their meadow, ignoring its flight,
Find themselves swallowed in mouthfuls of light.
But when the day's octopus blazes with red,
I plunge to the depths and go sweetly to bed.
Cods and scrods, all alive alive oh –
Life's dripping wet in the watery waters below…

From *Blooms of Dublin*

From Blooms of Dublin: A Musical Play based on James Joyce's Ulysses.

Act One

[No.1]

[*A Martello tower on the Dublin coast, temporary home to Stephen Dedalus and Buck Mulligan. Eight in the morning: Mulligan greets the day, and his house-mate, with his vision of a Hellenised Ireland.*]

BUCK   Let's turn this drab necropolis
MULLIGAN   Into an erotopolis –
            Every colleen Aphrodite,
            Casting off her woollen nightie.
            Our vices, drink and treachery,
            Replace with sunlit lechery.
            Put a ton of high explosive
            Under Mary and St Joseph,
            Exorcising gloom and sin –
            Let the pagan sun move in.

            Let's find some naked goddesses
            To deck our native odysseys –
            Every man his own Ulysses,
            Sailing seas of kicks and kisses.
            Groves where no lime or lemon is
            Can still have agapemones.
            Ouzo-drinking will spell *finis*
            To the wealth of Arthur Guinness.
            Down with the Irish pantheon,
            Turn the pagan sunshine on.

[No.2]

[*The same. Stephen and Buck have been joined by their English lodger, Haines. Stephen is haunted by memories of his dead mother; and by mothers of all kinds.*]

STEPHEN   Mother Ireland,
How many lice in your comb?
Bitter and bitchy though sweet of tongue,
The original sow that devoured her young.
I gave you my youth –
What more can I give?
For God's sake leave me alone and let me live.

Mother England –
Mistress in everyone's home.
Your Saxon language is all I've got,
Though my mouth finds it stranger than Hottentot.
You hold me in chains –
How can I forgive?
For God's sake leave me alone and let me live.

Sacra mater,
Weaving your web out of Rome –
You taught me virtue, but not so well
As you taught me to scream at the fires of hell.
I gave you my soul –
What more can I give?
For God's sake leave me alone, forget me,
Make believe that you never met me,
Mother! Leave me alone and let me live!

[No.5]

[*A Dublin street. Leopold Bloom is on his way home to Eccles Street after buying a pork kidney for his breakfast.*]

BLOOM   Today
It's the sixteenth of June today
And from morning till noon
The hours to come

Will add up to a humdrum
Sum-mer's day.
And yet
There's a feeling I seem to get –
I was having this dream
That let someone new
Sidle into my view:
We met.

What's the precognitive reason?
(If that's the right word)
What does this kind of thing presage?
(I don't get any sager)
Is it the glamour of the season –
Scents upon the breeze and
Hopes of early middle age?

It may
Just limp by in a routine way
Leaving nothing to say
But: one more dull summary:
One more dull summery day.

Plenty of fleshly exposure –
Necks and strawberries are red.
Buttocky peaches in a basket,
Racing on at Ascot,
In the royal enclosure
Ted.

We'll see
If there's anything else in store.
Let's be having it soon
This sixteenth of June
1904
A – D.

[No.7]

[The bedroom of Bloom's house. His wife, Molly, who is expecting a visit from her lover later in the day, laments the state of their marriage.]

MOLLY   It's your fault, Poldy, if I go to hell at all.
I'm doing badly but you've not done well at all.
If you treat me with such cold neglect,
What can you expect?
Living without loving till my chances are wrecked.

It's eighteen months since you did this or that to me
Or even laid a hand on my anatomy.
Don't you see that's how these things begin?
Forcing me to sin,
Giving it a welcome when it thrusts its way in.

But Jesus God, it's all the harm I ever did.
The priests get mad because it's what they never did.
Why did God make me the way I am –
Sweet as apple jam?
He just sees us do it without giving a damn.

But there's Our Lady, and she'll turn her back on me,
And that's when everything turns bitter black on me.

[A distant crack of thunder.]

God forgive me in my lonely tomb,
God forgive me at the crack of doom –
And although you
Are a disbelieving Jew,
God forgive you too,
Leopold Bloom.

[No.9]

[*Glasnevin cemetery; Paddy Dignam has just been buried. Bloom is overcome by morbid thoughts, and tries to shake them off with thoughts of life's pleasures.*]

BLOOM   Warm full-blooded life:
Women as shining as goddesses
Under the bustles and bodices,
Scent you could cut with a knife.
Warm full-blooded life:
Frilly silk drawers that have legs in them,
Omelettes with five hundred eggs in them,
Sherry and cream in the trif-
le.
The sun beating down on the bums of juvenile lovers,
Spiced plovers on toast and a roast under silvery covers.
Hot full-blooded nights:
Sin after sin and no nemesis,
Love on another man's premises,
Bosoms and blossoms and fights.
Warm full-blooded life:
Men full of lustful proclivities,
Dancing at parish festivities,
Each with another man's wife...

Act Two

[No.18]

[*The lying-in hospital, Holles Street, where Mrs Purefoy is giving birth to her latest. Medical students and their cronies drink and sing bawdy songs: including...*]

LENEHAN   Too many babies born
Too many babies born
A fertile womb is a thing of gloom:
Soon there won't be standing room.

STUDENTS   Copulation without population:
(as minstrels) This is the thing we all desire.

May God preserve the condom,
The pessary too, of course,
But hasten the day when we can slay
The life force at its source.
Masturbation means no procreation,
But hasn't got the true erotic fire.
Coitus interruptus is somewhat out of date,
And as for God's safe periods it's often hard to wait.
We ought to have a spermicide served hot upon a plate,
Then cop-u-late.

Copulation without population:
It's what every nation requires.
Why should we fill our houses
With messy squalling brats?
We need every square inch we can spare
For parrots, dogs and cats.
Pedication as a variation
Sets trilling all the hot erotic wires,
But love has only one true seat, so all the poets state,
A postlapsarian paradise for Adam and his mate,
With 'Raising Cain forbidden' written on the outer gate,
As well as COP –
(Why bring the police into it?)
ULA –
(United Lechery Association?)
TETETETE
Cop-u-late!

[No. 24]

[*Nighttown: the parlour of Mrs Cohen. Stephen, drunk like all the others, reminisces about his time in Paris.*]

STEPHEN   Paris is a lamp lit for lovers
Aloft in the wood of the world.
Blaze of noon or moonlight discovers
Miraculous duchies or earldoms
For lovers:
Paris uncovers

77

Riches never guessed at before,
But Paris is a bitch and a whore.

[*The whores are shocked at his rude language. He continues in a cancan tempo.*]

She'll tell you
What you want to listen to
And she'll sell you
What you want to buy.
She'll teach you
How to reach sublimities
Whose only limit is
The sky.

Teknophily, necrophily, cynophily, tragophily,
And modes of gerontophily
Too numerous to enumerate.
Flesh perfumed and flesh illumed
Or painted to seem new-exhumed,
And everything consumed
At a remarkable consumer rate.

[*End of cancan.*]

The river that the lover discovers
Is gilded and mother-of-pearled.
Its city is a lamp lit for lovers
Aloft in the wood of the world,
In the wood of the world.

First draft completed in 1971; produced for BBC Radio 3 and Radio Telefis
Eireann, and broadcast in the UK and Eire on 2 February 1982, the centenary of
James Joyce's birth. In *Earthly Powers*, which reprints some of these lyrics, *Blooms
of Dublin* is attributed to the composer Domenico Campanati and the librettist Sid
Tarnhelm: see chapters 72 and 73.

From *Will!*

Seven fragments from Will!, *an unmade Hollywood musical.*

WILL SHAKESPEARE
[*To Hamnet, on his knee*]
              Little son,
              When I look on thee
              I am filled with won-
              der such wonder can be –
              Part of me, yet no part of me,
              Wholly good, yet the wood of my tree.
              If I could
              I would live to see
              Fulfilled in me
              The man that I can never be,
              Born to property,
              Richly clad retainers about thee.
              Hawk on hand,
              You survey your land,
              Your acres shining in the summer's gold
              And I behold
              The glory of a name
              Restored to fame
              It had of old.
              Little son,
              If these things should be
              And I die before they are granted to thee,
              Think of me as he who carved them
              From the wood
              For the wood of my tree.

                        *

WILL
[*Seeing the 'W' of Cassiopeia in the sky*]
              My name in the sky
              Burning for ever,
              Fame fixed by fate

Never to die.
At least
I feast on that dream,
The gleam of gold, my fortunes mounting high.
To render my deed
More than pure fancy,
On lonely roads I must proceed,
My one companion a dream,
A seemly vision only I espy!
My name in the sky.

ANNE SHAKESPEARE (*née* HATHAWAY)
[*Singing in counterpoint to Will*]
          Will o' the wisp,
          A foolish fire,
          Leads fools to fall
          In mud and mire.
          Better by far
          The fire at home,
          Smoke in the rafter,
          Lamb's wool and laughter –

          Will o'the wisp,
          Do not desire
          To follow fame,
          That foolish fire.
          Better by far
          The fire at home,
          Fresh dawn on waking
          And fresh bread baking.
          A will o' the wisp
          Should not aspire
          To be a star.

*

WILL
[*Solo, after writing* Titus Andronicus, *contemplating his job as a popular dramatist*]
          Give the people what they wish:
          Something trite and tawdry,

Balladry and bawdry –
Give the people what they wish.

Give the groundlings what they crave:
Bombast and unreason,
Dog and bitch in season,
Prophecies of treason,
Rising from the grave.

Pillaging and ravishing and burning,
Royal heads and maidenheads
Presented on a dish,
In a pie.

Let them eat their stinking fish –
What they find delicious
Soon will seem pernicious.
When the time's propitious
That diet will cloy,
They will come to enjoy
What I wish
What I wish
What Iiiiiiiiiiiiiii
Wish.

*

WILL
[*To Hamnet, again*]

Tomorrow and tomorrow and tomorrow –
That makes three.
The first tomorrow is for me.
The second tomorrow – we.
The third tomorrow – thee.
I start with my poetic fame,
I then restore the family name,
And last of all I see
Thee –
Sir Hamnet, Lord Hamnet
The day after the day after tomorrow.
I pledge that these things shall be.

81

LUCY

[*The Dark Lady of the Sonnets is, in this version of Shakespeare's life, dark-skinned as well as dark-haired and -eyed; Lucy is a freed slave, brought up in Bristol and newly arrived in the capital of Elizabeth's England.*]

The white man's knavery
Sold me in slavery
To an unsavoury
Household.
I slept in an attic all
Foully rheumatical,
Bedbugged and cobwebbed
And mouseholed.

I slaved like the slave I was
Ripe for the grave I was
But I was brave, I was
Ready
For my master's remorse and my
Freedom of course and my
Carriage and horse and my
Monetary source
Safe and steady.
Now see me here in London,
Ready for revenge –
All England will be undone
From Carlisle to Stonehenge
On the dayyyyyyyy
I get my wayyyyyy.

I'll screw some sex into Essex,
I'll scourge Walter Raleigh's raw hide.
I'll make Francis Drake
Chase a duck on the lake
And eat Francis Bacon fried.
I'll inject the shakes into Shakespeare
And stick in the spear as well,
Wrench out Queen Bess's
Carroty tresses
And make her as bald as a bell.

Right under your gaze
I'm going to raise
Elizabethan hell.

*

BEN JONSON
Ale and Anacreon,
Beer and Boethius,
Sack and Sophocles, these
Please my heart more than the farting littleness,
Borborygmic brittleness,
Jokes and japes
Of the apes and jackanapes
One sees
Courting the great
At court, on estate –
Fleas!

*

LUCY
[*Spurning Will's protestations of love*]
Love, you say love, you say love?
All you're talking about
Is fleshly philandering,
Goosing and gandering,
Peacock and peahen stalking about,
Squawking about
Love,
He-goat, she-goat, mare and stallion,
Blowsy trull, poxy rapscallion.
You'd better know that my golden galleon
Is not for your climbing aboard
Of…

Written in 1968 for an unmade spectacular, originally entitled *The Bawdy Bard*, to
be produced by William Conrad and directed by Joseph L. Mankiewicz. Re-attrib-
uted to F.X. Enderby in *Enderby's Dark Lady, or No End to Enderby* (1984).

83

From *Trotsky's in New York!*

Three Songs from Trotsky's in New York! *(1980)*

1.

[Manhattan, 1917. Leon Trotsky, recently arrived in the United States, and accompanied by three male comrades, questions the revolutionary zeal of the American worker.]

TROTSKY   Amenities, amenities,
               He's got too many amenities.
               Obscene. It is
               Unclean. It is
               Not right.
               Facilities, facilities,
               It's loaded down with facilities,
               His billet. His
               Docility's
               A fright-
               ful nightmare.
               Phonographs and photographs
               In fine gilt frames.
               If you protest he only laughs
               And calls you names.
               How *can* the revolution come
               When he is stuffed up with chewing gum?
               His belly aches
               But it's with steaks
               And candy bars.
               Amenities, facilities
               Are killing all his abilities
               To reach up to the stars.
               We have a telephone.

BOKHARIN   That's bad?

TROTSKY   I never saw one in Petrograd,
               And what a revolutionary device

For sending vital messages,
While here this modern marvel is
For finding out the latest Wall Street price,
For ordering a double chocolate ice.
My children treat it as a pet
And play the numbers like roulette.
Last night –

CHUDNORSKY   Yes?

TROTSKY   You should have heard the calls they made.
A Mrs Elmore Schlitz who's deaf,
The Rockefellers' under-chef,
The chief of the Long Island fire brigade,
A girl who panders to men's lust,
The chairman of the Morgan Trust,
The Council for Industrial Expansion,
And then they had a cosy chat
With some big bug who's living at
A feudal palace known as Gracey Mansion.

Ah, luxuries, oh, luxuries,
New York's awallow in luxuries,
Its cocksure busy buck sure is
The king.
Commodities, commodities,
Baked beans and similar oddities
They worship like a god. It is
A thing
To bring one
To a state of palpitat-
ing wrath and rage,
Just seeing how they venerate
A living wage.
Each worker I've been looking at
Is just an overfed pussycat,
His only dream
Is double cream
And motor cars.
In every single facet he

Is thwarting his capacity

[*He breaks off the song and orates*]

to end the domination of the capitalistic monopolistic oppressors with their governmental lackeys and by erecting the classless society on a broad basis of economic equality to

[*He sings*]

> Grab the new moon as a sickle
> And hammer out a new cosmos
> Whose sparks shall be the stars.

2.

[*Against his principles, Trotsky has begun to fall in love with an attractive young comrade, Olga. Alone and agitated, he struggles against this powerful counter-revolutionary force.*]

TROTSKY   All through history
Mind limps after reality.
And what is reality? What's damned well there.
There's no mystery
In physical causality.
Life is simple. Desperately so. Beware
Of making it complex.
Sex, for instance, sex.
The need to breed, cell calling to cell.
Any set of cells will do as well
As any other set. And yet
This word *love, lyubof, Liebe, amore*
Sticks its ugly snout into the story.

All through history
Mind limps after reality.
And what is mind? A burst of electric sparks
Out of the clashing consistory
Of physical actuality.
Love's in the mind, but it isn't in Karl Marx.

86

Love's in William S.,
In Tolstoy, more or less,
And certainly in Dante Alighieri.
Pushkin? *Lyubof* flows like cream in a dairy.
Those poets aren't to blame. They came
Too soon to recognise their own confusion.
Love, we all know now, is a bourgeois illusion.

All through history
Mind limps after reality.
And what is reality? Good solid stuff.
There's no mystery
In physical causality.
Atoms, cells and bones and brains – enough.
The shape of a girl's face,
The thought of an embrace –
Irrelevant nugacities, totally and absolutely supererogatory –
So say Engels, Marx *et al.*,
No *die Liebe* in *Das Kapital*.
But today I find it necessary to say:
Keep away, girl, keep away girl, keep away!

3.

[*Trotsky's wife, Natalia, has been teaching a troupe of young New York dancers from a ballet school. They show off their new routine for his benefit.*]

DANCERS   A word is just a pen mark,
            A babble of sound.
            It means one thing in Denmark,
            Another in France,
            But all the world round
            People speak dance.

            A word is just a bubble
            Of air from the lungs.
            It's hardly worth the trouble
            To try to enhance
            Your knowledge of tongues:
            People speak dance.

With all due deference,
A bourgeois reference
Neatly makes the point.
The Bible tells of Babel,
But only dance is able
To put that joint out of joint.
You don't need French or Spanish
Or Russian or Greek.
Linguistic problems vanish
Away at a glance.
There's no need to speak
When you speak dance.

You don't need to call
On blah blah blah.
You can say it all
With an entrechat.
And if you have some-
thing else to say,
Let it come
In a fouetté.
Stop grunting over grammar
Like old-fashioned fools,
And make each tootsie hammer
Due south of your pants.
In all the best schools
Teachers teach dance.

The past indicative,
Labial fricative –
Don't these sound obscene?
Just throw away your syntax
And strew the floor with tin tacks
And be a Mexican bean.
So let's have no more anguish
With adverbs and verbs.
Let language go and languish,
Teutonic, Romance,
And the speech of the Finns and the Magyars
        and Croats and Serbs.
People speak dance!

From *A Clockwork Orange: A Play with Music*

Six Songs from A Clockwork Orange: A Play with Music *(1990).*

1.

[*Night in the Korova Milk Bar. Alex and his droogs sing 'The Nadsat Song'.*]

DROOGS   What's it going to be then, eh?
What's it going to be then, eh?
Tolchocking, drasting and kicks in the yarblockos,
Thumps on the gulliver, fists in the plott.
Gromky great shooms to the bratchified millicent,
Viddy the krovvy pour out of his rot.
Ptitsas and cheenas and starry babushkas
– A crack in the kishkas real horrorshow hot.

What's it going to be then, eh?
Deng in our carmans so no need for crasting
And making the gollybird cough up its guts.
Tolchocks and twenty-to-one in an alleyway,
Rookers for fisting and britvas for cuts.
What's it going to be then, eh?
As one door closes another one shuts.
Gavoreet horrorshow, but me no buts.

2.

[*The Korova Milk Bar. A singer, fresh from rehearsing with her colleagues at a nearby TV studio, sings the 'Ode to Joy' from the fourth movement of Beethoven's Symphony No. 9.*]

SINGER   Joy thou glorious spark of heaven,
Daughter of Elysium,
Hearts on fire, aroused, enraptured,
To thy sacred shrine we come.
Custom's bond no more can sever
Those by thy sure magic tied.

All mankind are loving brothers
Where thy sacred wings abide.

3.

[Alex's flat. His 'post corrective adviser', P.R. Deltoid, quizzes Alex about his wickedness.]

DELTOID   What gets into you all?
               Theological evil?
               The devil stalking the streets?
               The weevil in the flour of life?
               I repeat:
               What gets into you all?

ALEX   Let me explain to you, oh my brothers,
               As for him and the others,
               It's no good saying a word to them.
               It's never occurred to them that
               Energy's something built into a boy.
               But neither the church nor the state
               Has taught us how to create,
               So we've got to use energy to destroy.
               Destruction's our ode to joy.

DELTOID   What gets into you all?
               Is it biological? Drivel!
               It's unambivalent sin.
               It's the devil grinning within.
               God help us all.

4.

[Alex has been gaoled for murder. The warders set to work on him.]

WARDERS   Discipline, discipline,
               Let's have discipline,
               Give him a haircut and a shave.
               Courtesy, deference –

That's with reference
To the foul way you behave.
The names you call us
Quite appal us –
We're going to knock you into shape.
You're going to suffer,
You duffed up duffer,
You jabbering gibbering ape.

Discipline, discipline,
Real live discipline,
Like what you get in a war.
When we've got through with you,
What can they do with you?
Use you for swabbing the floor.
You're going to college
To get some knowledge
Of how to behave and how.
So here comes discipline,
Discipline, discipline,
Here comes discipline now.

5.

[*F. Alexander mourns the death of his young wife, the victim of Alex and his droogs.*]

ALEXANDER She was all things to me,
She was my body and my brain –
Her hair was sheaves of autumn,
Her smile was midsummer rain.
She was all springs to me,
The earth renewed every day.
The leaves come green in April,
Though they
Fall in the fall and burn.
She will not return.

Often in dreams I hear her
(I'm standing near her)

– She shakes her head.
'The futility of anger,
The sin of vengeance:
How can these profit the dead?'
But if they were here –
I'm living still –
My living will
Would seek to break, to rend, to kill –
Useless, useless, as she said.

She was all springs to me.
The earth renewed every day.
The leaves come green in April,
Though they
Fall in the fall and burn
She will not return.

5.

[*Finale: the whole company sings to the tune of the 'Ode to Joy'.*]

CHORUS   Being young's a sort of sickness,
Measles, mumps or chicken pox.
Gather all your toys together
Lock them in an iron box.
That means tolchocks, crasting, dratsing,
All the things that suit a boy.
When you build instead of busting,
You can start your Ode to Joy.

Do not be a clockwork orange,
Freedom has a lovely voice.
Here is good, and there is evil –
Look on both, then take your choice.
Sweet in juice and hue and aroma,
Let's not be changed to fruit machines.
Choice is free but seldom easy –
That's what human freedom means!

From *Mozart and the Wolf Gang*

1. Act One

[*An indeterminate hall in the Vienna palace of the Prince Archbishop Hieronymus Colleredo of Salzburg. Servants, male and female, scrub, clean, polish, bring logs for the fireplace. Mozart, the court musician, warms himself gloomily.*]

SERVANTS   Humble humble humble humble
                Servants of his princely grace,
                Fashed and fagged we groan and grumble,
                Outcasts of the human race.
                Humble humble humble humble
                Burdened beasts that know their place.
                See us fumble, see us stumble,
                And the bitter bread we crumble
                And the skilly that we mumble.
                Dare to look us in the face,
                Helots of his high disgrace.
                Hear our empty bellies rumble
                Treble
                Alto
                Tenor
                Bass.

MOZART   Slavishly begot,
(*tenor*)   Slavery's your lot.
                Luggers in of logs,
                You are less than dogs.
                Dogs at least are fed
                Bones as well as bread.
                Lowly born,
                Accept my scorn.

SERVANTS   Humbly humbly humbly humbly
                May we ask if it's a crime
                Dumbly dumbly dumbly dumbly
                (Yes, we know that's not a rhyme)
                To be born beneath a star

Burning with malignant fire?
Humbly dumbly we enquire
Who the hell you think you are.

MOZART   I was not born beneath a star. I
Am a star.
Leaning across the heavenly bar, I
Fell too far.
The crown of music on my head was
Knocked awry.
Fingering keys to earn my bread was
By and by
Ordained to be the life I led and
Still must lead.
So will it go till I am dead and
Dead indeed.

SERVANTS   Humbly humbly humbly humbly
May we ask you what you mean?
All you said was soft and crumbly;
Words should cut as keen and clean
As the whip the gruff and grumbly
Major-domo, rough and rumbly,
Lays on us to vent his spleen.

MOZART   I played the harpsichord at four
And scribbled symphonies at five.
I played and played from shore to shore.
I laboured – never bee in hive
Buzzed harder at its sticky store –
To keep the family alive.
For Leopold my father swore
I'd fiddle, tinkle, sweat and strive
Until the name the family bore
Should gather honour and survive
Two centuries and even more.
But infant prodigies arrive
At puberty. Must we deplore
Our beards and balls, though noses dive
And patrons stay away or snore?
I serve his highness now, contrive

To play the postures of a whore.
Too meanly paid to woo or wive,
I sink and sink who used to soar.
Grant me your pity, friends, for I've
Heard slam that ever open door,
Been forced to kiss the nether floor,
Who once kissed queens –

SERVANTS   Kissed queens?

MOZART   Kissed queens.
Not any more, not any more.

My scullion companions, I've run out of hope. Also rhymes.
To work. I hear steel heels and the crack of a whip.

[*Enter Major-Domo and the Prince Archbishop's private secretary.*]

SERVANTS   Humble humble humble humble
Servants of his princely grace,
Hear our empty bellies rumble
Treble
Alto
Tenor
Bass.

*

2. Act Two, Scene Two

[*A billiard room in the imperial palace. Mozart, Salieri and Gluck drink a toast to the discipline of counterpoint*]

THE THREE   The cruelty of counterpoint,
The toothache of the fugal,
The twinge in each creative joint.
The public loves the frugal
Enjoyment of a bugle,
But we must slave at counterpoint.

At four- and five-part counterpoint,

The dovetail of the voices,
The midnight potions that anoint
The engine that rejoices
In stringency of choices,
The creaking wheels of counterpoint.

GLUCK   My fugues were ash and rubble.

MOZART   I never had much trouble.

SALIERI   (And that's the bastard's trouble.
                I'll prick the bastard's bubble.)

GLUCK   The real or tonal answer –

MOZART   Mere dances to a dancer.

SALIERI   (I'll trip this flighty dancer.
                God, let him die of cancer.)

THE THREE   The mastery of counterpoint,
                The mystery of counterpoint,
                Subjection to its rules
                Will make your rating mount a point
                In the pedantic schools
                Where analytic ghouls
                Probe strictly at strict counterpoint
                The strictest strictest counterpoint,
                The fools.

3.

[*The same, shortly afterwards. Gluck has suddenly died; the Chamberlain announces Mozart's appointment as Gluck's successor as* Kammermusicus – *but at a far lower stipend. Mozart objects to this slight, and is reprimanded for his presumption.*]

EMPEROR   Learn decorum, sir. I may
                Remove this honour right away.
                It is not fitting to discuss

What a mere Kammermusicus
Receives from the imperial fisc.
In a less liberal day you'd risk
Your head and not a mild rebuke
From one prepared to overlook
Your lowly ignorance of the sort
Of manners proper to a court.

MOZART   With all due deference, sire, I bow
And even grovel.
But is not Europe changing now?
In hut and hovel,
In German *Schloss* and French *château*
Sensitive noses
Scent something in the wind and know
It is not roses.
Rousseau, Voltaire and Beaumarchais
Have warned already.
The autocrats have had their day.
I hear the heady
And steady music of the march
Of common people
Ready to fell the imperial arch,
Tear down the steeple.
May not musicians join the throng,
At last respected,
The honoured founts of honest song,
No more dejected
As mere discardable machines
Wound up to tickle
The ears of emperors, kings, queens
Whose tastes are fickle?
I realise that what I say
Seems rank sedition,
But let me hail it while I may –
The coming dayspring of his day:
The free musician!

Untitled libretto; published in *Mozart and the Wolf Gang*, 1991.

From Sophocles, *Oedipus the King*

CHORUS

STROPHE

To Thebes, the city of light, from out of the gold
Shrine of the golden god the word has come.
It is not a word of deliverance that is told.
Fear cleaves our hearts, fear renders us dumb.
Hear, O hearer, healer of Delos, hear,
Tell us in our fear what you will do.
Will it be something new?
Will it be something old as the wheeling year?
Daughter of hope, we call on you.

ANTISTROPHE

There are three divinities
Whose task it is
To avert
Adversities.
Artemis, Artemis,
Daughter of the father of
The gods, who
In majesty but with a special love
Sits above our city.
Next, from her sister Athena, we
Seek pity. Last
From Phoebus, lord of the bow, the far
Shooter, we ask
Aid in our task.
O, in the past
You drove away fire, plague, famine
     from the state.
Be great as then,
Help us again.

Our sorrows are so many they cannot be told.
Sickness holds the land. The hand is numb
That drives the useless plough. The shepherd's fold
Is striken. The city soon will become
Empty of life, the ship is beached, its wood
Rotting, rotten. No seed takes hold
In the earth or in the womb. Like flocks of birds
The hopeless leave the city, seeking some good
On the shore of an alien god. Words,
Words of prayer are all that is left to us,
But our mouths grow cold.

ANTISTROPHE

Death in the streets,
Children lying
Dead in the streets, spreading
Contagion of death.
The breath of the mourners,
The suppliants, freezes
On the altar. Alter
Our condition, Golden Athena,
Golden Apollo, grant
Remission to our pain.
The night wind,
The morning breeze is
Sour with pain.
Once you listened.
Listen again.

STROPHE

There is war, but not a war of brazen shields,
No clash of armour lifts the heart. Our war
Is with the god of war himself. He strikes our fields,
Our homes, a savage god, a god of fire, whose roar
Is louder than the cries of the dying. O Zeus,
Exile the war god to some northern shore,
For we can no longer abide the tortured night,

The agony of the morning. Let your bright
Lightning strike him, turn loose
Your steeds of thunder under whose fiery feet
He will be beaten and crushed and seen no more.

ANTISTROPHE

Slay him, Apollo,
You of the golden bow.
Artemis, slay him, flashing
In torchlight
Over our hills. And you,
Bacchus, splashing
Wine in boistrous revelry,
With your torch of pinewood
Scorch him, burn him,
Send him screaming away,
The enemy,
The god whom all the gods
Abhor and loathe to see,
Restoring joy
To the bright day!

Written 1972; first performed at the Guthrie Theater, Minneapolis, Minnesota, directed by Michael Langham, with music by Stanley Silverman.

From Griboyedov, *Chatsky*

Three extracts from Chatsky, *a verse comedy in four acts by Alexander Sergeyevich Griboyedov.*

From Act One

[*After some three years away from Russia, the brilliant, sardonic, idealistic young writer Chatsky has just returned home to Moscow, and presented himself at the house of his old flame Sophie, expecting a more amorous welcome than she seems prepared to give.*]

CHATSKY   The sun's up. But your radiance casts a fierier glow
On this your servant, kneeling at your feet –
Figuratively speaking. Come, a kiss. We meet
After an endless parting. Were you not
Expecting me? Not one solitary jot
Of pleasure? Just a cold trickle of surprise?
Heat in your cheeks but not much in your eyes.
One would think a week, even a day,
Had passed, and we had bored the time away.
Love, I expected love. Swiftly I come
Wrapped in a traveller's delirium,
Forty-five hours without a wink of sleep.
Five hundred miles, my carriage buried deep
In snow or lashed by blizzards, soaked in rain,
Wheels broken – mended – broken. And my brain
Dazed with desire to get to you. Devotion
That's earned at least a modicum of devotion.

SOPHIE   Mr Chatsky, I'm very pleased to see you.

CHATSKY   That's something. But if you were me and me you,
Would that be enough? How's one supposed to act
When one is really pleased? Is it a fact
That I've exposed myself to lethal immersion
In icy rivers just for my own diversion?

LIZA [the maid]   Why, sir, you should have eavesdropped seconds ago.

We were talking about you. Isn't that so?

SOPHIE   Not only now. We talk about you always.
See you in the shops, in streets, in hallways,
Follow your shadow, look for your image in
Travellers from foreign parts, ask if they've been
Where you were, asked captains of foreign ships
If they have seen your post-chaise on their trips.

CHATSKY   I'd like to believe that, so believe I do.
Blessed is the believer. What's not true
Can still be – cosy. Well, well, back again
In Moscow. With you – you as you were then,
Or not? Oh Lord, how innocent we were,
Appearing, disappearing – here, then there,
Romping around that table – and that chair.
There sat your father, there that old madame
Playing at piquet, while we used to cram
Ourselves in that dark corner, safe secluded,
Until a creak, a croak, a cough intruded.

SOPHIE   Nursery days.

CHATSKY   And now you're grown.
Radiant. A beauty of your own.
Fascinating, fit to fire a poet,
Inimitable, and by God you know it.
That's why you're cold, stand-offish. You compel me
To ask if you're in love. Come on now, tell me.
Don't stop to think up something nice and plausible.
Don't get so flustered.

SOPHIE   Really, it's impossible
Not to get flustered when you stare like that,
Firing off questions.

CHATSKY   What else can I stare at
But lovely you? Moscow, of course, invites
Stares, as do our high-class Muscovites.
Gossip and love affairs. Tomorrow's ball,
The two last night – it soon begins to pall.

Moscow, beautiful Moscow, at a pinch'll
Do, I suppose, but God, it's so provincial.

SOPHIE   You've seen too much of the world. This running down
             Of your native land. Is there a better town?

CHATSKY   The best place is where none of us cretins are.
             But never mind. How is your dear papa?…

From Act Two

[*Chatsky argues angrily with Sophie's reactionary father, Famusov, who compares the rising generation unfavourably with their illustrious forebears. His tirade concludes.*]

FAMUSOV   …You, you modern puppies. Get away.

CHATSKY   All right, all right – it may be as you say.
             The world's gone soft. Because it no longer suits
             Our generation to go licking boots
             And arses to have sinecures and honours
             And cast-iron penny medals showered upon us.
             There was no choice then. Lose your head in war,
             In peacetime let it scrape along the floor,
             And turn God's truth into political error.
             That was the age of grovelling and terror,
             Disguised as zeal to serve the swine on top.
             You think Russia's changed? No. Full stop.
             We won't disturb your uncle's rotting carcase.
             It's ghastly, probing that primeval dark, as
             Paupers grope in garbage, to recall
             How some would give worlds for the chance to fall
             To raise a royal laugh. Christ, what ambition.
             There are still plenty with that disposition.
             But now a whiff of shame sweetens the air.
             We thumb our noses at the pigs up there.

FAMUSOV   Oh God, he's a subversive.

CHATSKY   A wind's blowing.

There's air to breathe. We know now where we're going.
We prick the shibboleths like toy ballons,
Don't rush to join the regiment of buffoons.

FAMUSOV   Oh, my God –

CHATSKY   Kicking their heels in anterooms,
Fetching chairs, sick of the sick perfumes
Of haughty patronesses – seen, not heard,
Cackling at a pseudo-witty word
Filched from some poet left to rot in jail.

FAMUSOV   You're preaching liberty, you know.

CHATSKY   I fail
To see why I shouldn't. The real people are
Those who think a little and live far
From metropolitan corruption, people who
Do the work they know they have to do
For the work's sake, not the disdainful others.

FAMUSOV   Soon you'll be saying that all men are brothers....

From Act Three

[*To the amazement and disgust of the assembled company at an aristocratic
soiree, Chatsky – already branded as a near-lunatic – rails against the
Muscovite fashion for all things French.*]

CHATSKY   I've just met a little Frenchman from Bordeaux,
Puffed up, rotund, one of the tribe who know
Their own superiority, had quite an assembly
Around him, while he told how he was trembly
With apprehension, off to barbarous Russia.
But all he found was civility, such a crush, a
Crowd, a cram of hospitality.
I'm still in la belle France, oui, mes amis.
Nothing but French – the food, the conversation,
The ladies' dresses. All this imitation.

'France, ah, lovely France!' they were elated,
These young Princesses, reared on Francomania.
Russia, Siberia, Latvia, Lithuania –
All rubbish. Me, I stood some way away
And meekly, audibly, began to pray
That the good Russian god might strike and slay
This damned civility, these xenophiles,
Who lard their lardy jowels with smirks and smiles
Whenever anywhere but here is mentioned.
Abroad. Ah, Europe. Europe is the French and
Any nation that's been Gallicised.
They call me 'bigot', one of the despised
Race of the reactionaries when I say
That Russia should pursue the Russian way.
We drop our customs, ancient holiness,
Our noble language and our northern dress,
Scraping our chins, powdered like babies' bums,
Aping each little crowing cock who comes
From France. 'Can you translate Mademoiselle?
Madame? Such terms cannot be rendered well
Into the barbarous Russian tongue.' Oh God,
I say, try 'Miss or Mrs'. They: how odd,
Oh, what a joke. It's not enough to scoff –
They laugh their wretched Frenchified heads off.
I think of a reply. They go away.
Anyone who has anything to say
Home-brewed, true Russian, from the Russian soul,
The Russian soil, can go and dig a hole,
Shove himself in it. Let him be so bold
As wish to tell the world – lo and behold.
Lo and behold –

ALL   Mad!

Translated 1992; first performed by the Almeida Theatre Company, 11 March 1993.

From Rostand, *Cyrano de Bergerac*

Three extracts from Cyrano de Bergerac, *a verse play by Edmond Rostand (1897).*

1.

[*Act One. A Parisian theatre, 1640. The Vicomte de Valvert has made a less than dazzlingly witty remark about the size of Cyrano's nose. Angered, but perfectly self-controlled, Cyrano launches into a rhetorical tour-de-force, showing Valvert up as an inarticulate boor.*]

VALVERT   That thing of yours is big, what? Very big.

CYRANO [*most affably*]   Precisely what I was saying.

VALVERT   Ha!

CYRANO   Nothing more?
Just a fatuous smirk? Oh, come, there are fifty-score
Varieties of comment you could find
If you possessed a modicum of mind.
For instance, there's the frank aggressive kind:
'If mine achieved that hypertrophic state,
I'd call the surgeon in to amputate.'
The friendly: 'It must dip into your cup.
You need a nasal crane to hoist it up.'
The pure descriptive: 'From its size and shape,
I'd say it was a rock, a bluff, a cape –
No, a peninsula – how picturesque!'
The curious; 'What's that? A writing desk?'
The gracious: 'Are you fond of birds? How sweet –
A Gothic perch to rest their tiny feet.'
The truculent: 'You a smoker? I suppose
The fumes must gush out fiercely from that nose
And people think a chimney is on fire.'
Considerate: 'It will drag you in the mire

Head first, the weight that's concentrated there.
Walk carefully.' The tender-hearted swear
They'll have a miniature umbrella made
To keep the rain off; or for summer shade.
Then comes the pedant: 'Let me see it, please.
That mythic beast of Aristophanes,
The hippocampocamelelephunt,
Had flesh and bone like that stuck up in front.'
Insolent: 'Quite a useful gadget, that.
You hold it high and then hang up your hat.'
Emphatic: 'No fierce wind from near or far,
Save the mistral, could give that nose catarrh.'
Impressed: 'A sign for a perfumery!'
Dramatic: 'When it bleeds, it's the Red Sea.'
Lyric: 'Ah, Triton rising from the waters,
Honking his wreathed conch at Neptune's daughters.'
Naïve: 'How much to view the monument?'
Speculative: 'Tell me, what's the rent
For each or both of those unfurnished flats?'
Rustic: 'Nay, Jarge, that ain't no nose. Why, that's
A giant turnip or a midget marrow.
Let's dig it up and load it on the barrow.'
The warlike: 'Train it on the enemy!'
Practical: 'Put that in a lottery
For noses, and it's bound to win first prize.'
And finally, with tragic cries and sighs,
The language finely wrought and deeply felt:
'Oh that this too too solid nose would melt.'
That is the sort of thing you could have said
If you, Sir Moron, were a man of letters
Or had an ounce of spunk inside your head.
But you've no letters, have you, save the three
Required for self-description: S.O.T.
You have to leave my worsting to your betters,
Or better, who can best you, meaning me.
But be quite sure, you lesser feathered tit,
Even if you possessed the words and wit,
I'd never let you get away with it.

DE GUICHE [*apprehensive now*]   Come away, viscount, leave him.

VALVERT [*suffocating with rage*]

Arrogant, base
Nonentity, without even a pair of gloves
To his name, let alone the ribbons and lace
And velvet that a man of breeding loves.

CYRANO I'm one of those who wear their elegance
Within. To strut around and dance and prance
Got up like a dog's dinner – that's not me.
Less of a fop than you, sir, I may be,
But I'm more wholesome. I have never wandered
Abroad without my insults freshly laundered,
Or conscience with the sleep picked from its eye,
Or honour with unragged cuffs. Why, my
Very scruples get a manicure.
When I walk out I like to be quite sure
I smell of nothing but scrubbed liberty
And polished independence. You will see
My soul a ramrod as if corseted
And as for ribbons, all I ever did
Brave and adventurous flutters from my clothes.
With spirits high, twirled like mustachios,
Among the false and mean I walk about,
And as for spurs, I let the truth clash out.

VALVERT [*spluttering*] You –

CYRANO Gloves, you mentioned gloves. You have me there.
I have this one left over from a pair.

[*He produces it from his pocket, and a wretched ragged fingerless thing it is.*]

An old, old pair. Its fellow I can't trace.
I think I left it in some viscount's face.

VALVERT (*throbbing with rage*)
Cad, villain, clod, flatfooted bloody fool!

[*Cyrano, unmoved, doffs his hat and bows low.*]

CYRANO And *I'm* Cyrano Savinien-Hercule
De Bergerac.

2.

[The same. Cyrano and Valvert fight their duel; as they exchange swordplay, Cyrano improvises a fighting ballade, matching his actions to his words.]

CYRANO   I bare my head from crown to nape
           And slowly, leisurely reveal
           The fighting trim beneath my cape,
           Then finally I strip my steel.
           A thoroughbred from head to heel,
           Disdainful of the rein or bit,
           Tonight I draw a lyric wheel,
           But, when the poem ends, I hit.

           Come and be burst, you purple grape,
           Spurt out the juice beneath your peel.
           Gibber, and show, you ribboned ape,
           The fat your folderols conceal.
           Let's ring your bells – a pretty peal!
           Is that a fly? I'll see to it.
           Ah, soon you'll feel your blood congeal,
           For, when the poem ends, I hit.

           I need a rhyme to hold the shape –
           Gape, fish. I'm going to wind the reel.
           My rod is lusting for its rape,
           The sharp tooth slavers for its meal.
           There, let it strike. Ah, did you feel
           The bite? Not yet. The vultures sit
           Until the closing of the deal.
           The poem ends, and *then* I hit.

[He stands solemnly to attention.]

        [ENVOI:]

           Prince, drop your weapon. Humbly kneel,
           Seek grace from God in requisite
           Repentance. Now – I stamp the seal.
           The poem ended – and I hit!

[He dispaches the viscount neatly.]

3.

[End of Act Five. Fifteen years later: 1655. The garden of the convent to which Roxane retreated after the death in battle of her supposed lover, Christian. Cyrano is bitterly impoverished, and fatally ill. At the eleventh hour, Roxane has suddenly discovered that it was Cyrano who provided the eloquent words of love for Christian, and so is really the man she has always loved. But the revelation comes just as Cyrano is drifting in and out of the delirium which precedes death. In a brief moment of clarity, he declaims his own epitaph.]

CYRANO   Philosopher and scientist,
                      Poet, musician, duellist,
                      And voyager through space.
                      A sort of controversialist,
                      Whose wit kept to a charted track
                      But sped at a great pace,
                      A lover too, who seemed to lack
                      The luck in love of other men –
                      Here lies Hercule-Savinien
                      De Cyrano de Bergerac,
                      Nothing, everything, nothing again –
                      Sunk now, without trace.

                      I have to leave you. Sorry. I can't stay.
                      That lunar shaft is – waiting to carry me away,
                      A punctual and impatient sort of
                      Engine.

[He falls back in his chair. The sobbing of Roxane recalls him to reality. He looks at her. He strokes her veiled hair.]

                      I would not ask that you mourn any the less
                      That good brave Christian blessed with handsomeness,
                      But, when the final cold sniffs at my heart
                      And licks my bones, perhaps you might impart
                      A double sense to your long obsequies,
                      And make those tears, which have been wholly his,
                      Mine too, just a little, mine, just a –

ROXANE   My love, my only love –

[*Cyrano, shaken again by fever and delirium, brusquely raises himself. The others move forward to help him, but he brushes them away. He sets his back against the tree trunk.*]

CYRANO   Not here, oh no, not lying down. Let
No one try to help me – only this
Tree. He's coming. He's coming. Already
I feel myself being shod in marble,
Gloved in lead.
[*With joy*]
               Let him come, then.
He shall find me on my feet –
[*He draws.*]
My sword in my hand.

LE BRET   Cyrano!

CYRANO   There he is, looking at me, grinning
At my nose. Who is he
To grin, that noseless one?
What's that you say – useless, useless?
You have it wrong, you empty brain pan.
You see, a man
Fights for far more than the mere
Hope of winning. Better, far better
To know that the fight is totally
Irreperably incorrigibly in vain.
A hundred against – no, a thousand.
And I recognise every one, every one of you.

[*He lunges at the air again and again.*]

All my old enemies – Falsehood, Compromise,
Prejudice, Cowardice. You ask for my
Surrender? Ah no, never, no never. Are
You there too, Stupidity?
You above all others perhaps were predestined
To get me in the end. But no, I'll
Fight on, fight on, fight –

[*He swings his sword again, then stops breathless. During his last speech he falls into Le Bret's arms.*]

> You take everything – the rose and the laurel too.
> Take them and welcome. But, in spite of you,
> There is one thing goes with me when tonight
> I enter my last lodging, sweeping the bright
> Stars from the blue threshold with my salute.
> A thing unstained, unsullied by the brute
> Broken nails of the world, by death, by doom
> Unfingered – See it there, a white plume
> Over the battle – A diamond in the ash
> Of the ultimate combustion –

[*Roxane kisses his forehead. He opens his eyes, recognises her, smiles.*]

> My panache.

[*Curtain.*]

Written for the Royal Shakespeare Company, 1983. Later used as the source of sub-titles for Jean-Paul Pappeneau's *Cyrano* (1989).